D0297637

Bicton College
25701

The Clue Books

FRESHWATER ANIMALS

Gwen Allen
Joan Denslow

illustrations by
Derek Whiteley

OXFORD
UNIVERSITY
PRESS

Oxford University Press, Walton Street, Oxford OX2 6DP

OXFORD NEW YORK TORONTO
DELHI BOMBAY CALCUTTA MADRAS KARACHI
PETALING JAYA SINGAPORE HONG KONG TOKYO
NAIROBI DAR ES SALAAM CAPE TOWN
MELBOURNE AUCKLAND

and associated companies in
BERLIN IBADAN

FIRST PUBLISHED 1970
REPRINTED 1974, 1976, 1979, 1981, 1982, 1984, 1987, 1990, 1991

PRINTED IN HONG KONG

This is a book about animals that spend all or part of their lives in fresh water, in lakes, ponds, rivers, and streams. They can be found under stones, on leaves and stems of plants, or swimming in the water.

In order to use this book you will need real animals. The illustrations below show the kinds of nets you will need when you are collecting them.

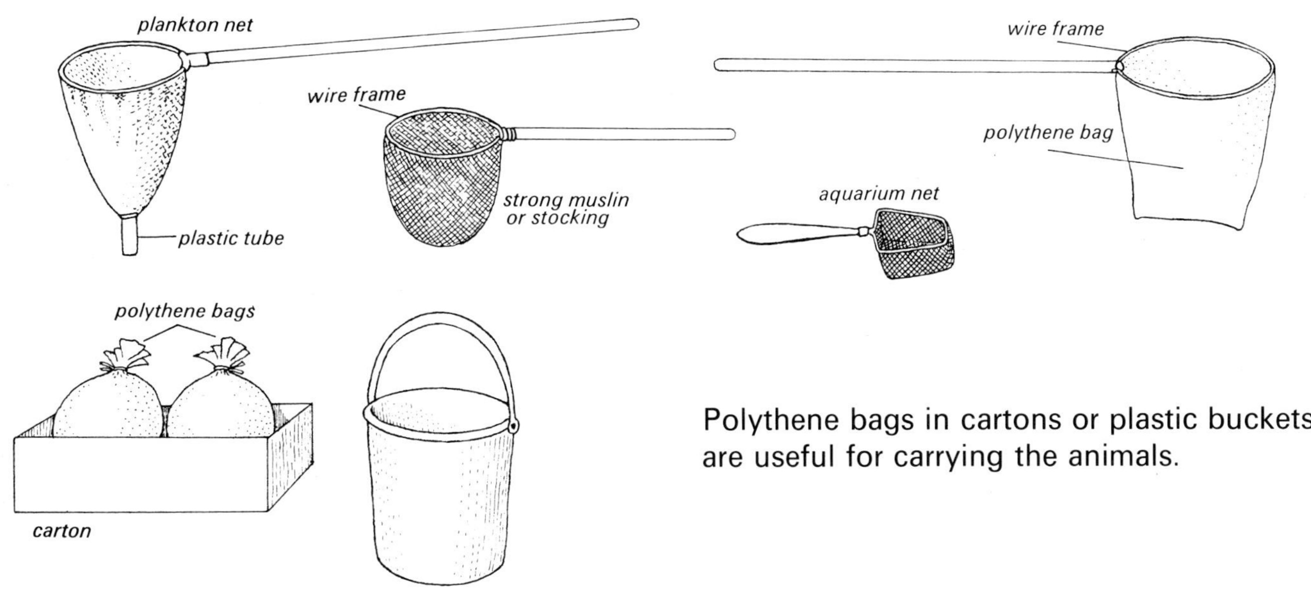

Polythene bags in cartons or plastic buckets are useful for carrying the animals.

You will have to prepare several aquariums before you collect the animals (see pages 54, 55).

When you have finished observations on the animals in your aquarium, return them to the place where you found them, or to somewhere like it.

The full-grown size of the animals in this book, from pages 26–50, is shown by a line ⊢——⊣ beside each drawing. When the line looks like this ⊢→——⊣ it means that the same kind of animal may be as small as this ⊢→ or as large as this ⊢——⊣.
If there is no line it means that the animal has been drawn life-size or larger than life-size.
The full-grown size of larger animals is shown beside the illustration.

All animals that live in fresh water hatch from eggs (see pages 22–25).

Some eggs hatch into young that do not at first look like their parents; at this stage of their life they are called LARVAE.

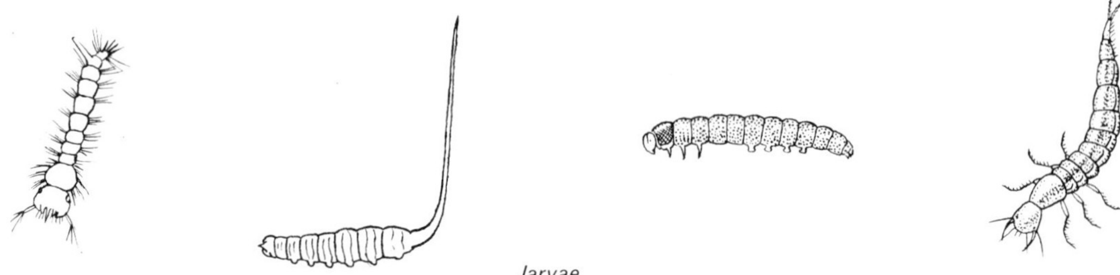

larvae

Insect larvae eat a great deal of food and grow quickly; they shed their skins every time they grow too big for them. When the larva is full grown it stops eating and changes into a PUPA. During this stage it changes into an adult.

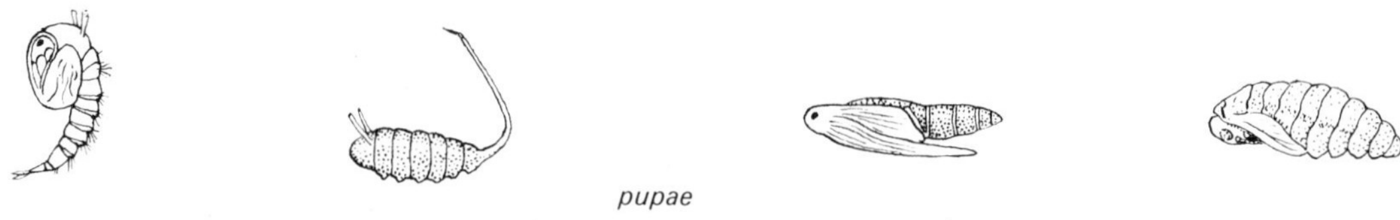

pupae

When the change is complete the pupal skin bursts and the adult insect emerges.

insects emerging from pupae

Larvae of frogs, toads, and newts are called TADPOLES; these gradually change into adults (see page 25).

tadpoles

Some eggs hatch into young that look like their parents, but their wings are not fully grown. These animals are called NYMPHS; they eat a great deal of food and shed their skins when they grow too big for them. Each time they shed their skins (moult) their wings can be seen to be larger.

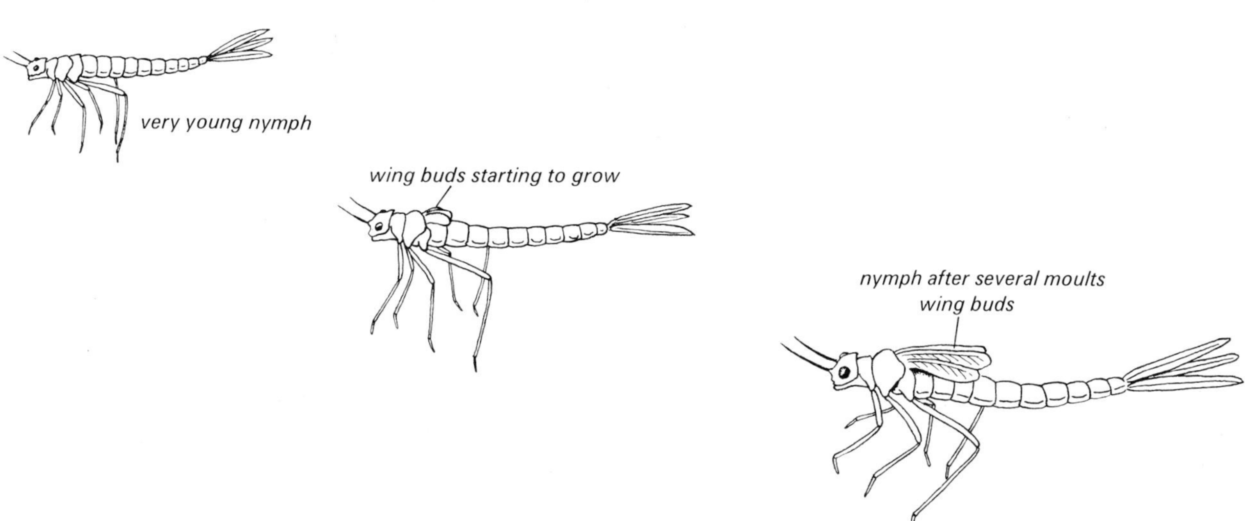

Some eggs hatch into young that look like their parents.

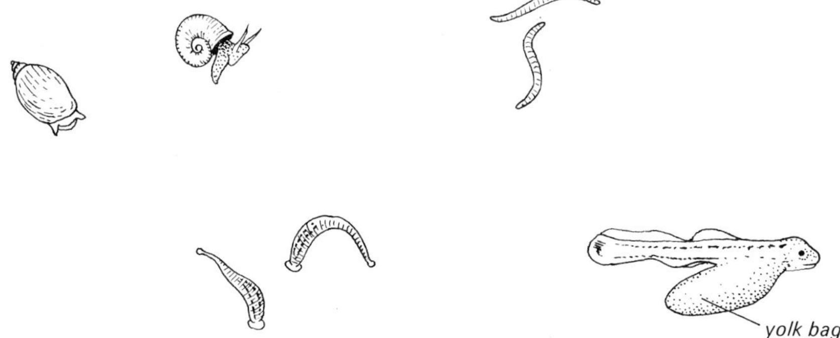

When you have found an animal, the clues on pages 6–23 will help you to name it. Begin by using the clues on pages 6, 7, and 8.

Look carefully at the animal. If it is small, use a magnifying lens or microscope. Find the clue that fits it, then turn to the page given for the next clue. Repeat this until you find its name or group.

CLUES TO NAMING ANIMALS THAT LIVE IN FRESH WATER

Most of the drawings of parts of animals in the clues are larger than life size.

---

1. If the animal has four legs and hairless skin without scales, it is an AMPHIBIAN.

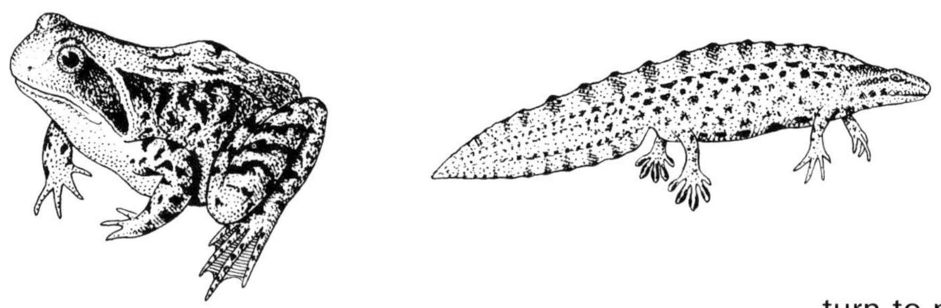

turn to pages 25, 26, 27

---

2. If the animal has fins and usually a scaly skin, it is a FISH.

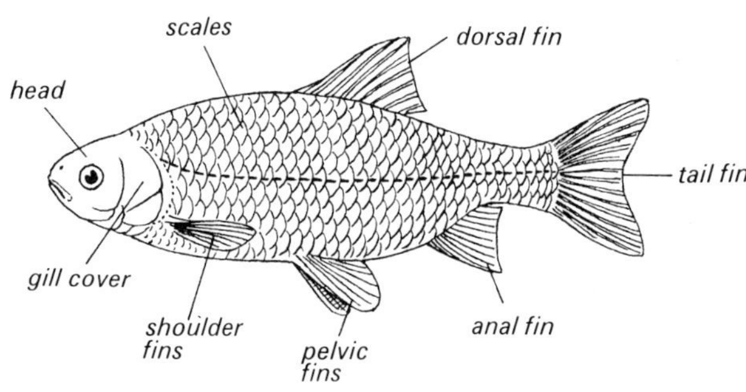

turn to page 9

3. If the animal has six jointed legs, three parts to its body (head, thorax, abdomen), and wings, it is an adult INSECT.

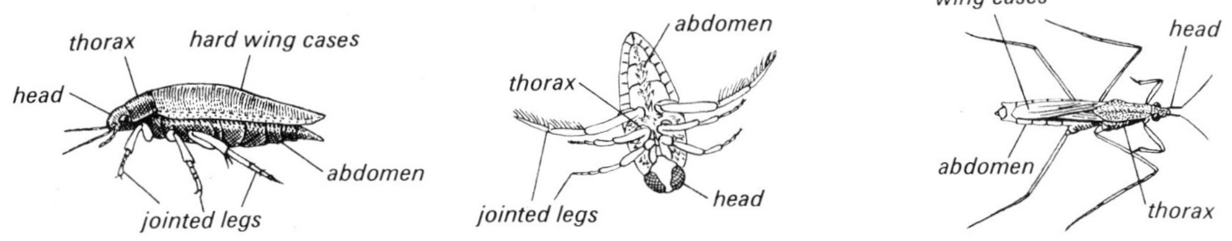

turn to page 12

4. If the animal has six jointed legs and wing buds, it is a young INSECT called a NYMPH (see page 5).

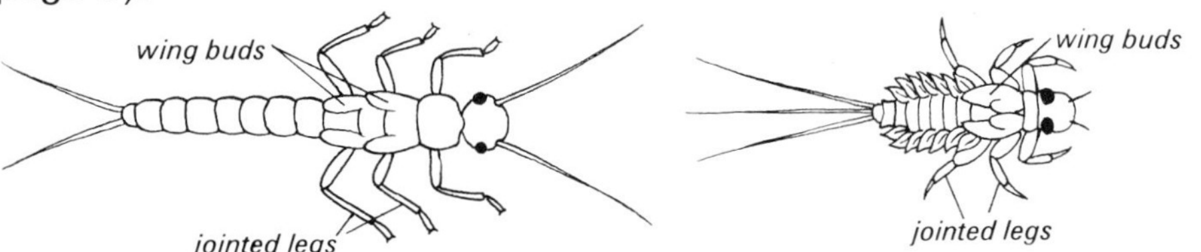

turn to pages 12, 13

5. If the animal has six jointed legs, but no wings or wing buds, it is probably a young INSECT called a LARVA (see page 4) or a wingless adult INSECT.

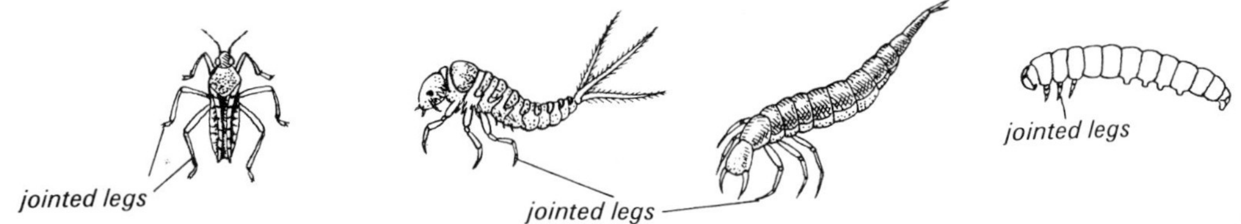

turn to pages 14, 15

6. If the animal has eight jointed legs, only one or two parts to its body and no wings, it belongs to the SPIDER group.

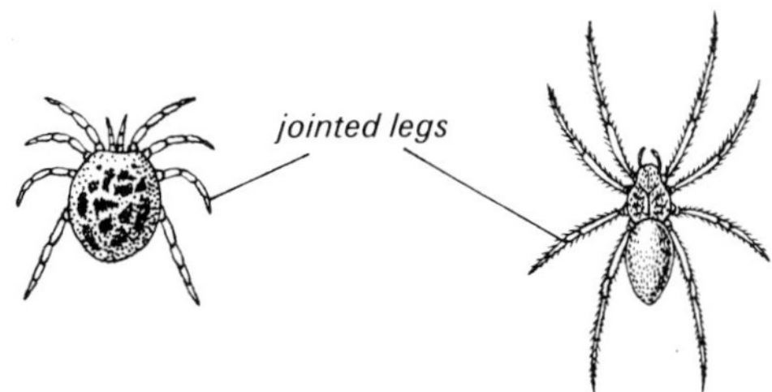

turn to page 15

7. If the animal has ten or more jointed legs but no wings, it belongs to the CRAB group.

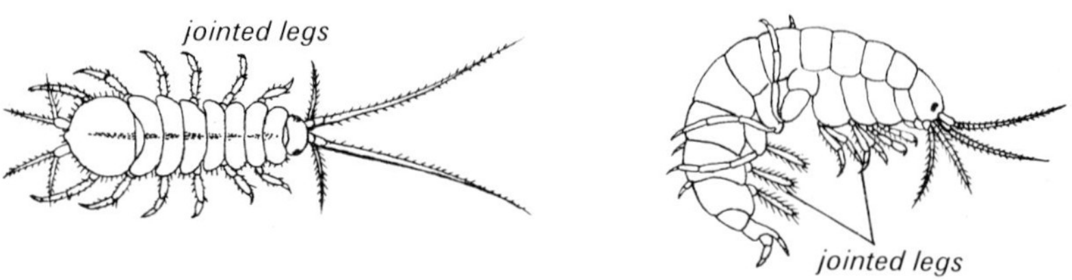

turn to page 16

---

8. If the animals are very small (⊢⊣), move quickly, and have legs that can be seen only if looked at under good magnification, they are WATERFLEAS, belonging to the CRAB group.

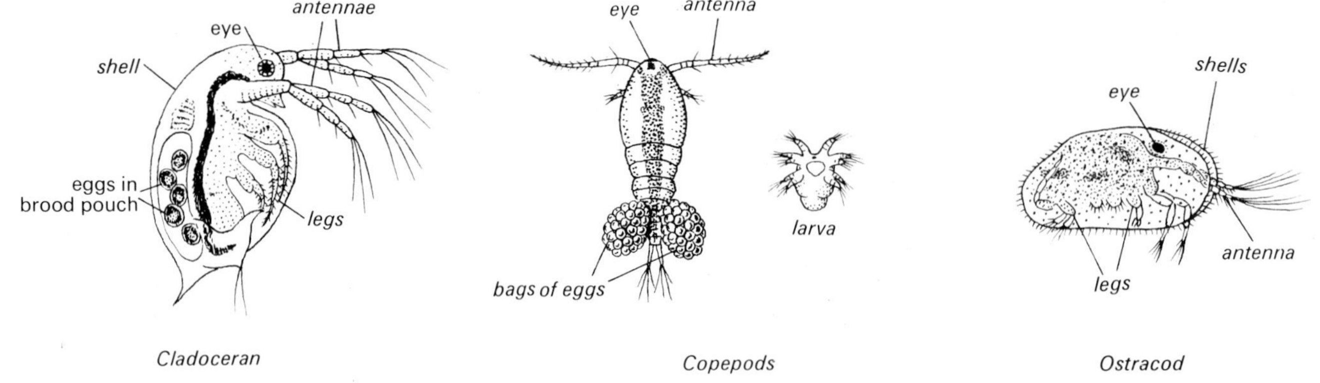

Cladoceran *Copepods* *Ostracod*

turn to page 45

---

9. If the animal has no legs or wings and is not less than 1 cm long

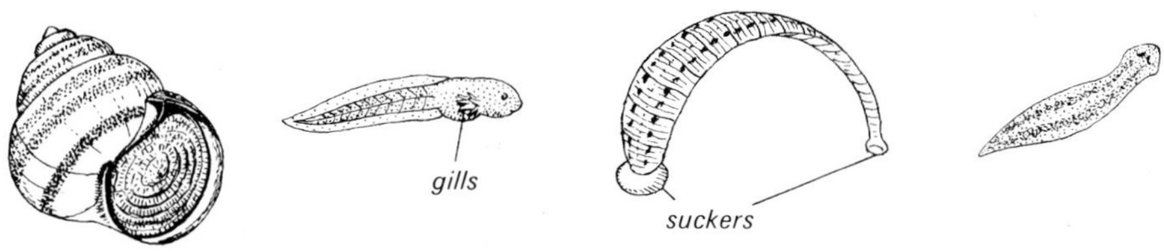

turn to page 17

---

10. If the animal does not look like any of these, examine it carefully, using a strong lens or microscope if necessary, and turn to pages 18, 19.

From page 6, clue 2

1. If the fish has a single fin on its back

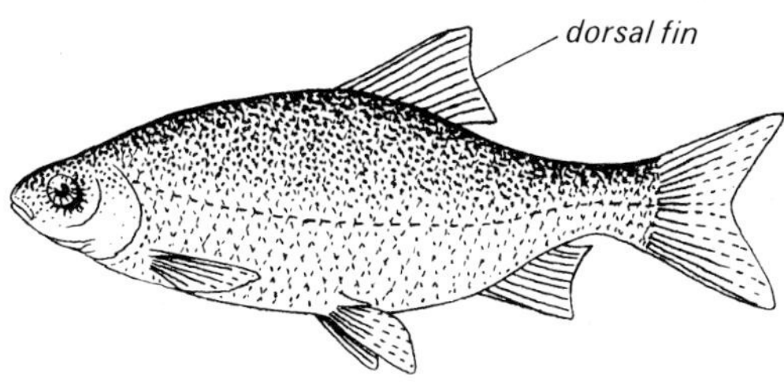

turn to page 10

---

2. If the fish has two fins on its back

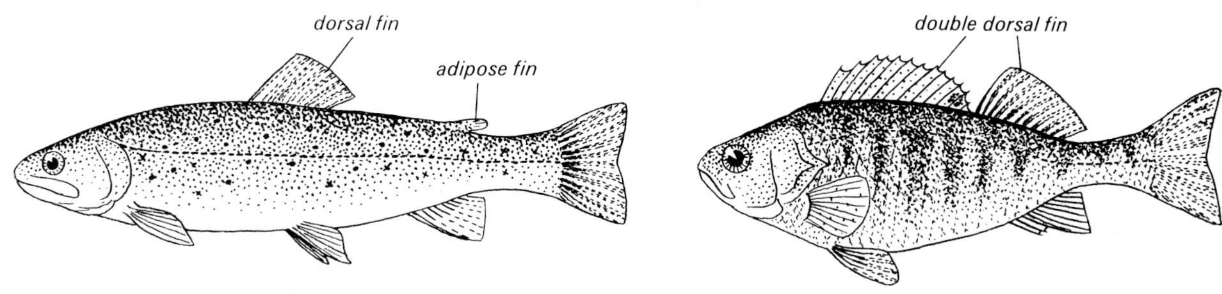

turn to page 11

---

3. If the fish has a single fin most of the way round its body, it is probably an EEL.

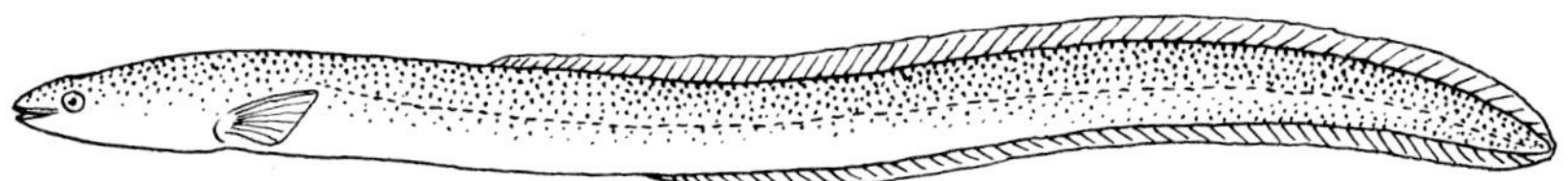

turn to page 29

From page 9, clue 1

1. If the fish has six barbels, it may be a LOACH.

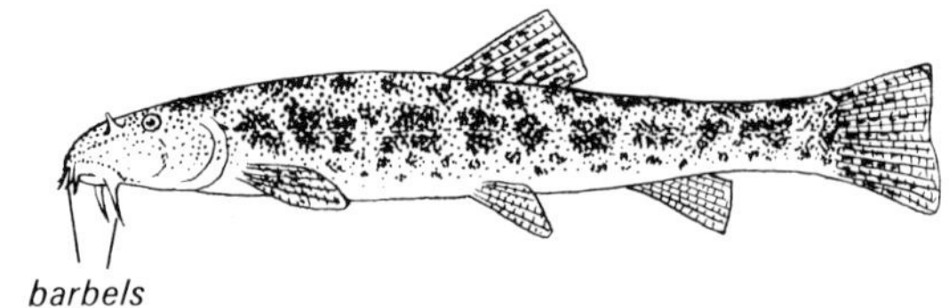

turn to page 29

---

2. If the fish has four barbels, it may be a BARBEL or CARP.

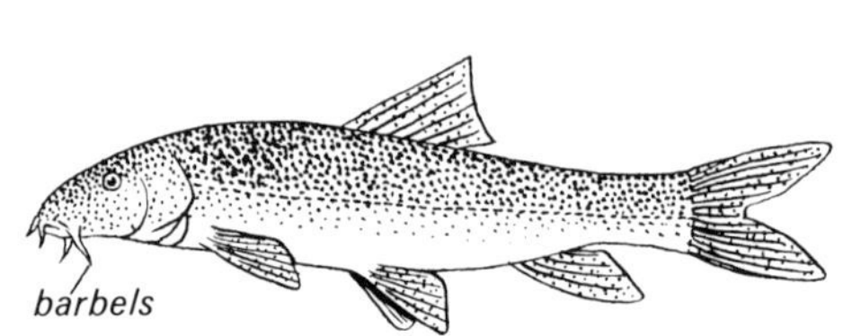

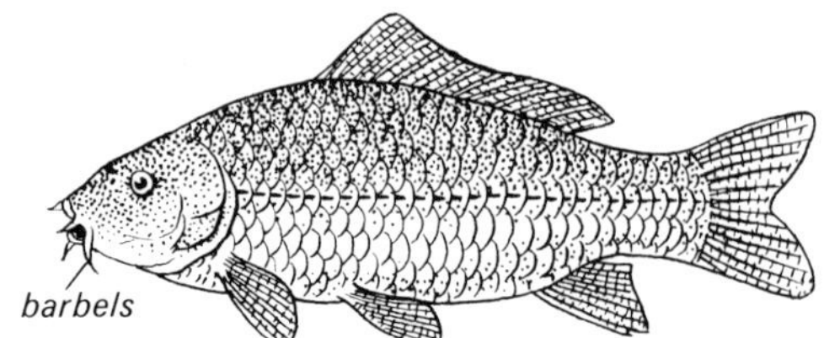

turn to page 31

---

3. If the fish has two barbels, it may be a GUDGEON or TENCH.

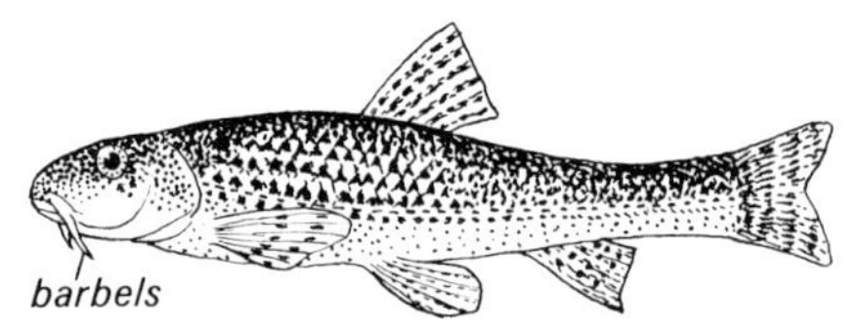

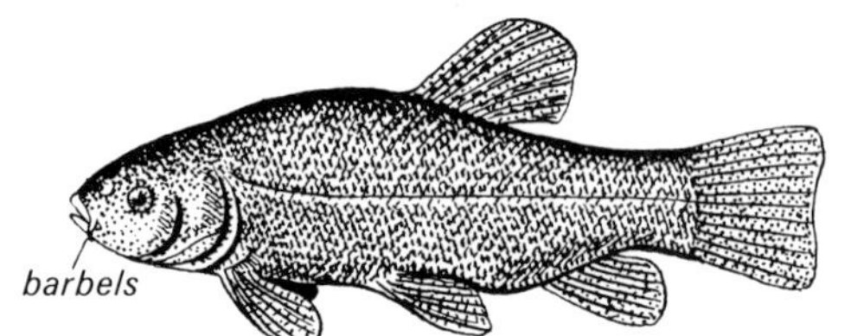

turn to page 31

---

4. If the fish has no barbels and no teeth on its jaws, it may be a MINNOW, CHUB, DACE, or RUDD.

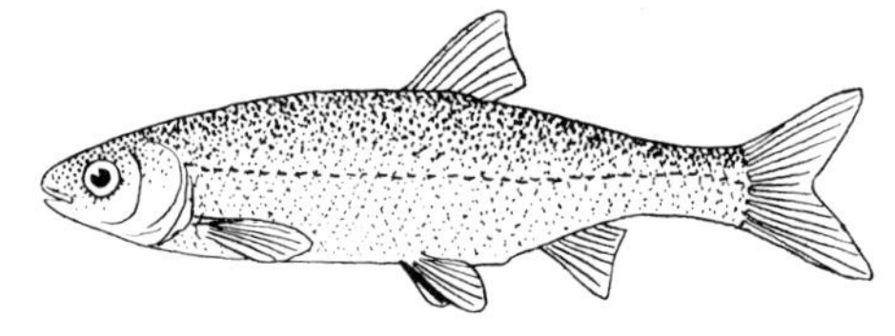

turn to page 31

---

5. If the fish has no barbels and strong upright teeth in its jaws, it may be a PIKE.

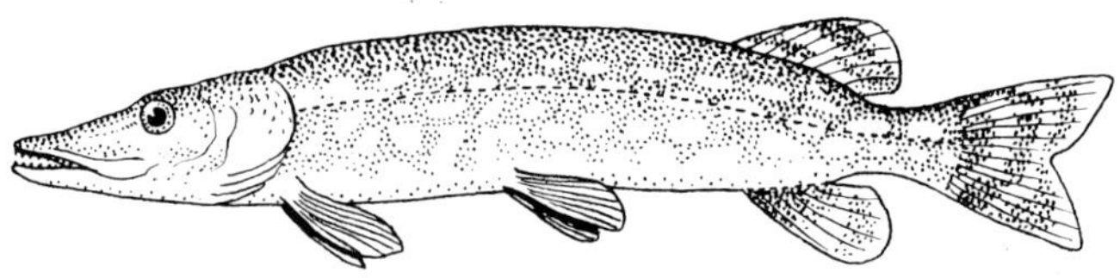

turn to page 29

From page 9, clue 2

1. If the fish has a large dorsal fin and a small adipose fin, it is a TROUT.

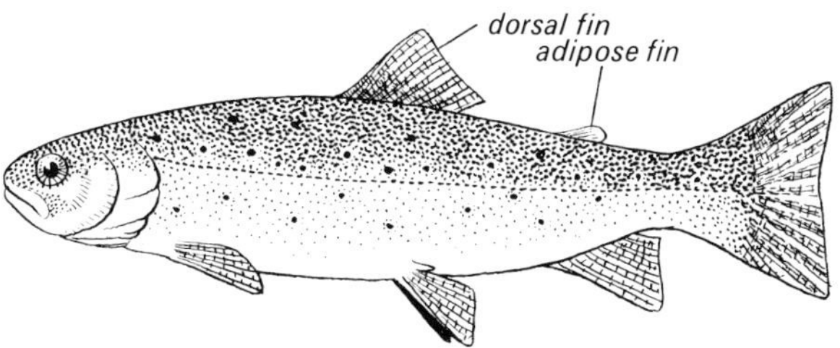

turn to page 29

---

2. If the fish has dorsal fins of similar size, the front one spiny, it is probably a PERCH.

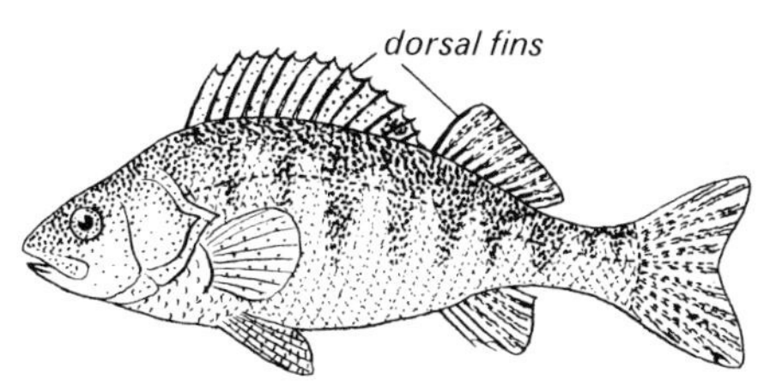

turn to page 29

---

3. If the fish has spiny dorsal fins of different sizes and no scales on its body, it is probably a BULLHEAD.

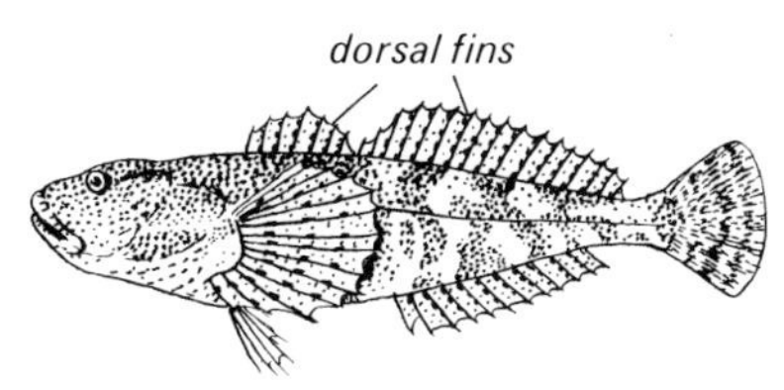

turn to page 29

---

4. If the fish has a front dorsal fin with three or ten spines, it is a STICKLEBACK.

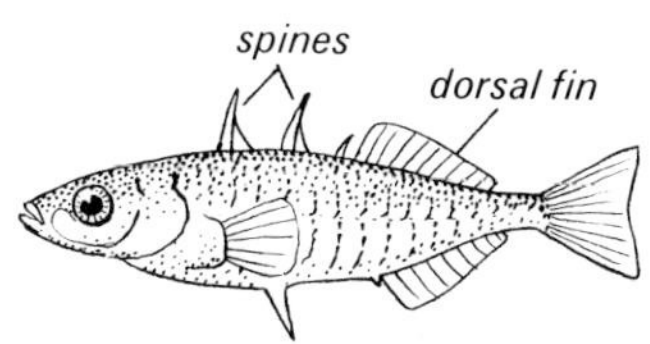

turn to page 29

From page 7, clue 3

Look carefully at the hard wing cases.

1. If the animal has hard wing cases and a shield-like part (scutellum) on its back, it is one of the BUGS.

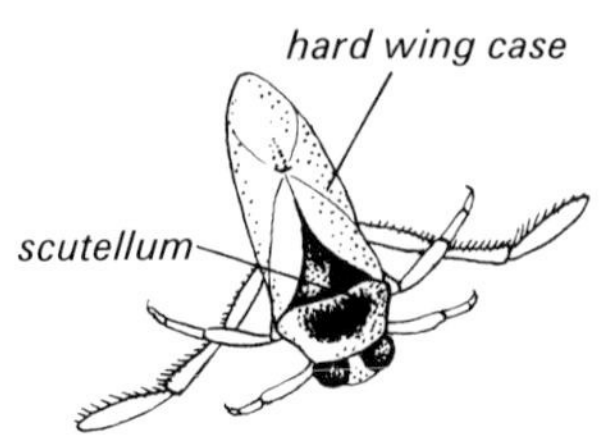

turn to pages 32, 33

---

2. If the hard wing cases cover most of the animal's body, it is one of the BEETLES.

turn to pages 34, 35

From page 7, clue 4

Using a magnifying lens look carefully at the animal.

1. If the animal has leaf-like gills along the sides of its body and three tail filaments, it is probably a MAYFLY NYMPH.

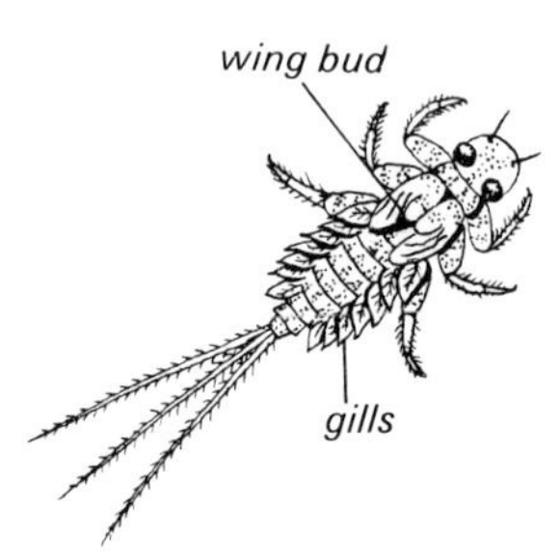

turn to pages 36, 37

---

2. If the animal has a slender body, three tail filaments, very large eyes, and jaws on the end of a mask (see clue 4), it is probably a DAMSELFLY NYMPH.

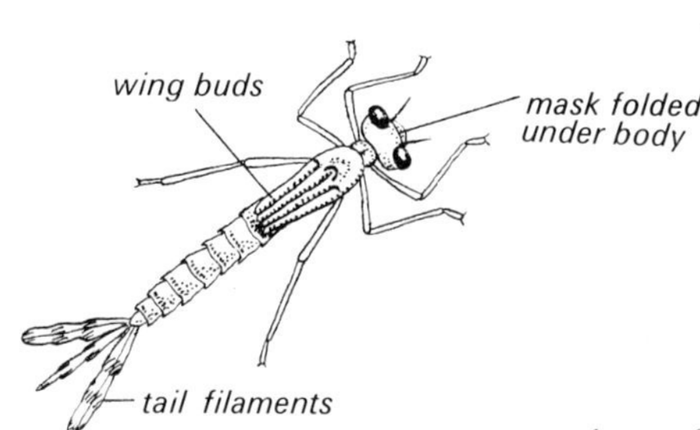

turn to pages 36, 37

From page 7, clue 4

3. If the animal has a slender body, two tail filaments, and long antennae, it is probably a STONEFLY NYMPH.

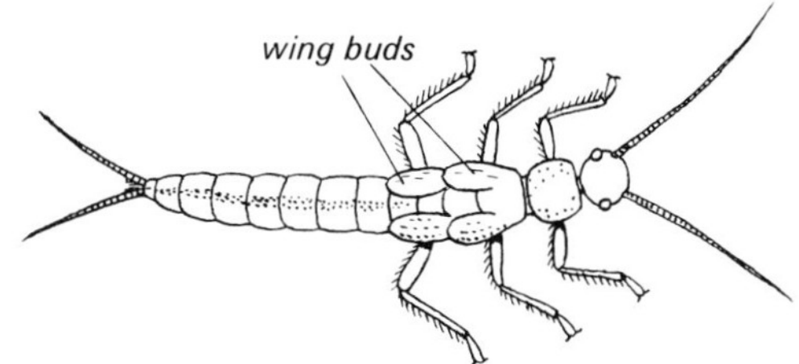

turn to page 37

---

4. If the animal has a stout body, very large eyes, and jaws on the end of a mask, it is probably a DRAGONFLY NYMPH.

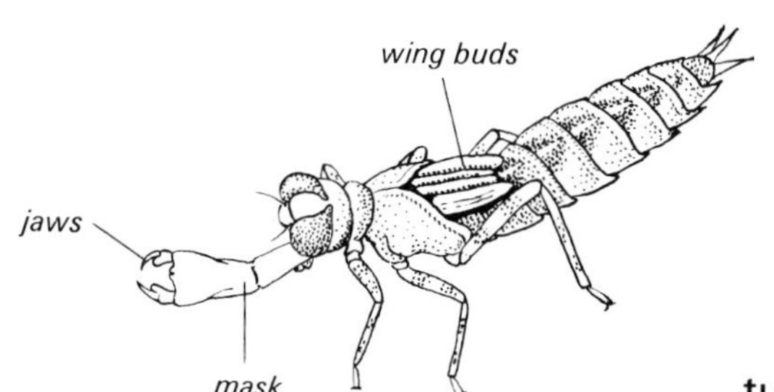

turn to pages 36, 37

---

5. If the animal's hind legs are longer than the others, and are used for swimming, it may be a WATER BOATMAN.

turn to pages 32, 33

---

6. If the animal is small, has long legs, and moves quickly over the surface of the water, it may be a POND SKATER, WATER CRICKET, or WATER GNAT.

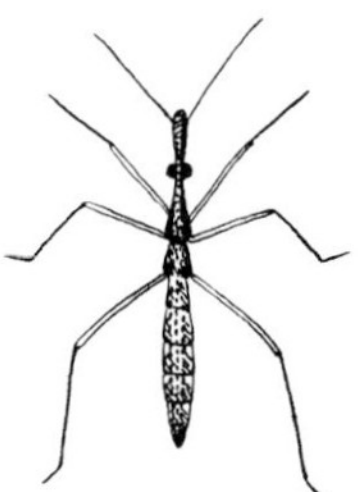

turn to pages 32, 33

From page 7, clue 5

1. If the animal has jointed gills along the sides of its body, it is probably an ALDER-FLY LARVA.

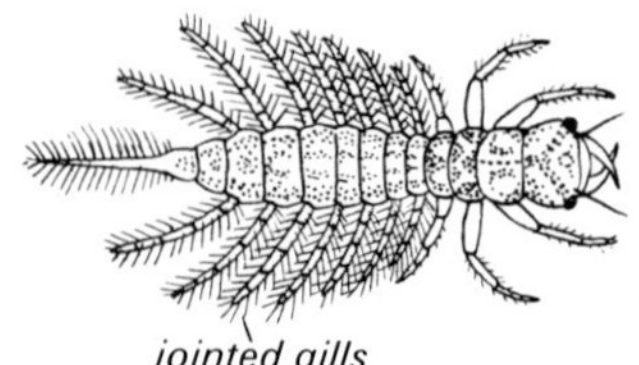

turn to pages 38, 39

---

2. If the animal has gills along the sides of its body and four tail filaments, it may be a WHIRLIGIG BEETLE LARVA.

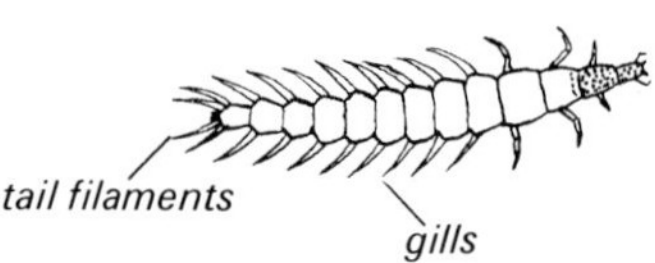

turn to pages 34, 35

---

3. If the animal has three tail filaments and looks like this, it is probably a SCREECH BEETLE LARVA.

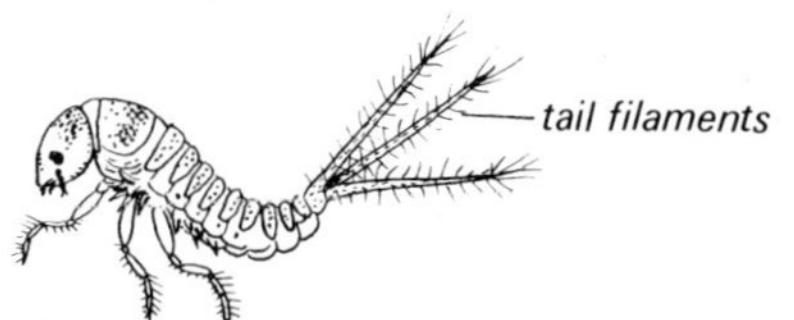

turn to pages 34, 35

---

4. If the animal has a long body, large biting jaws, and two short tail filaments, it is probably a WATER BEETLE LARVA.

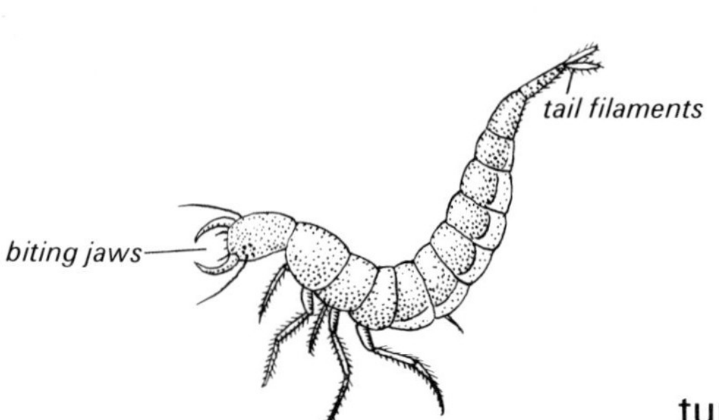

turn to pages 34, 35

From page 7, clue 5

5. If the animal lives in a tube made of leaves, sticks, or stones, it is a CADDIS LARVA.

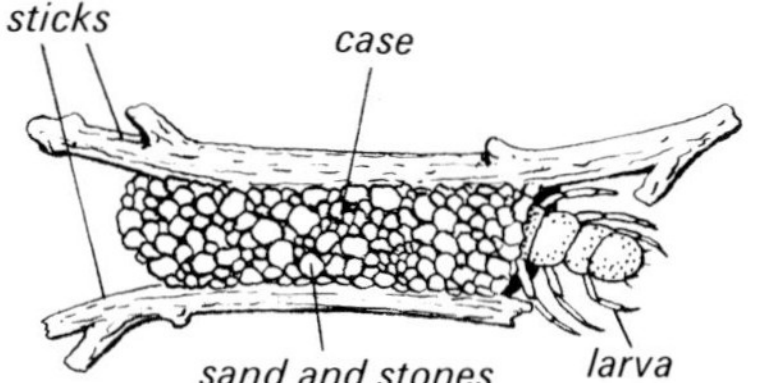

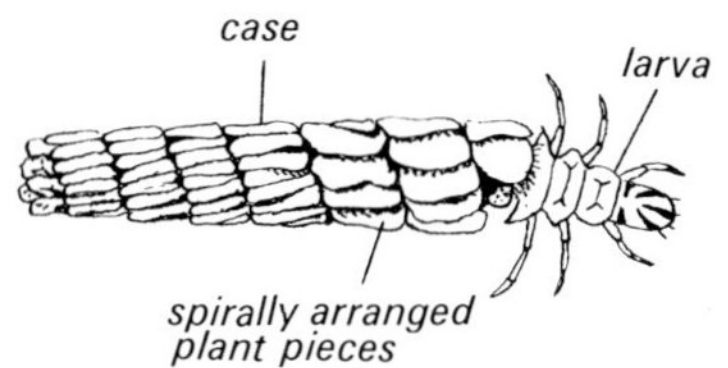

turn to pages 38, 39

---

6. If the animal is a caterpillar, and lives in a tube of silk attached to the underside of a floating leaf, it is a CHINA MARK MOTH LARVA.

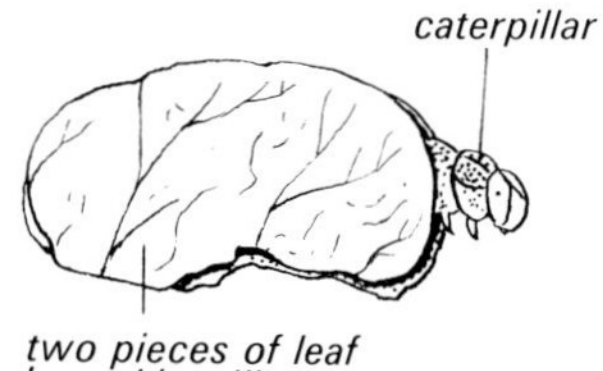

turn to pages 39, 42

From page 7, clue 6

1. If the animal has two parts to its body, with its legs attached to the front part, it is a SPIDER.

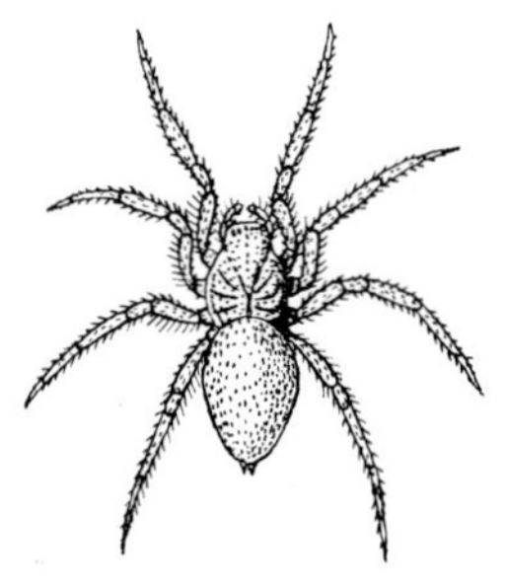

turn to pages 46, 47

---

2. If the animal is very small, swims quickly, and appears to have only one part to its body, it is a WATER MITE.

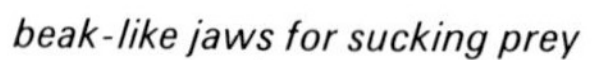

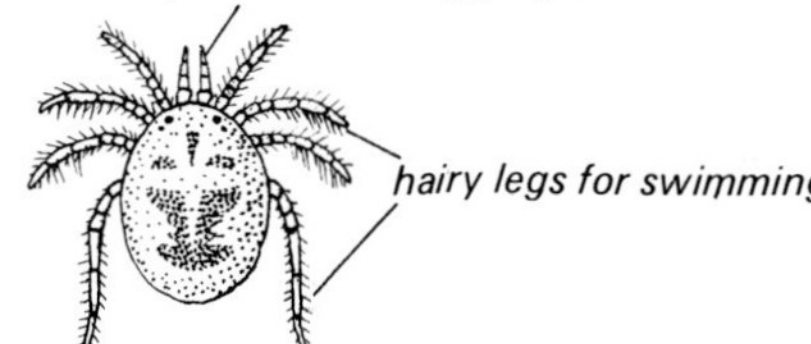

turn to page 47

From page 8, clue 7

1. If the body of the animal is flattened from side to side, it is a FRESHWATER SHRIMP.

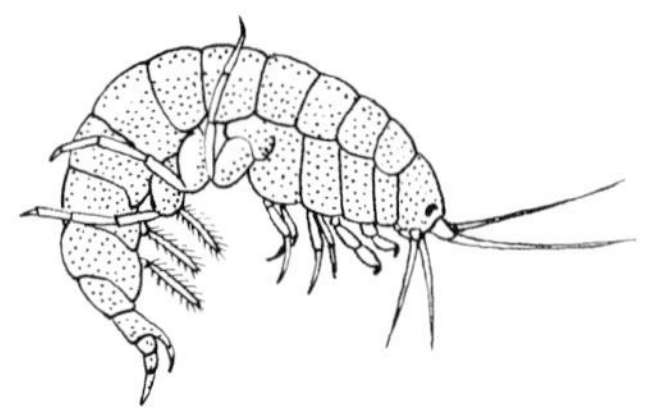

turn to pages 44, 45

---

2. If the body of the animal is flattened from top to bottom, it is a WATER SLATER.

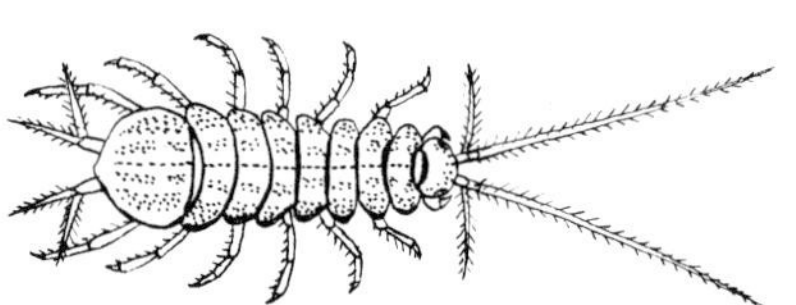

turn to pages 44, 45

---

3. If the body of the animal is transparent and flattened from top to bottom, it is probably a FISH LOUSE.

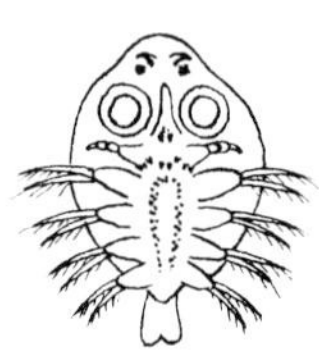

turn to pages 44, 45

---

4. If the animal is large, and has five pairs of legs, the first pair having long pincers, it is a FRESHWATER CRAYFISH.

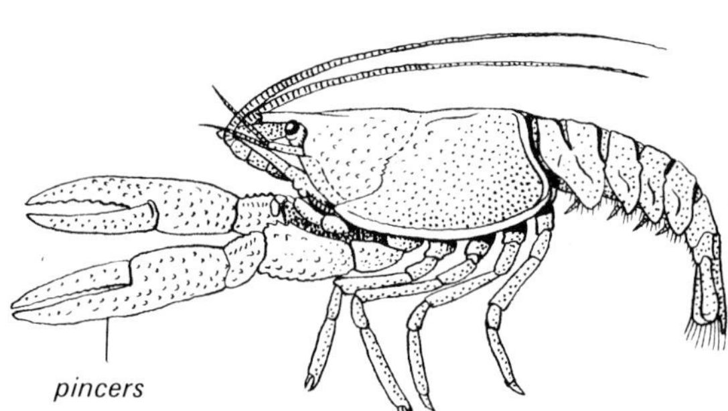

turn to pages 43, 45

From page 8, clue 9

1. If the animal has one or two solid shells, it belongs to the SNAIL GROUP.

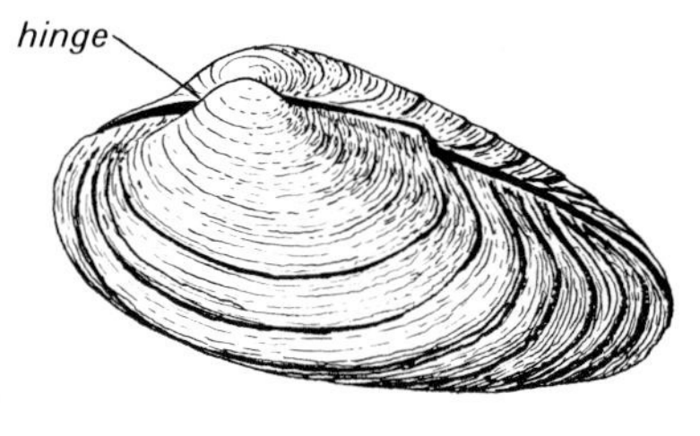

turn to page 20

---

2. If the animal looks like this, it is probably a TADPOLE.

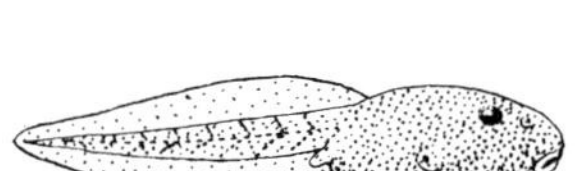

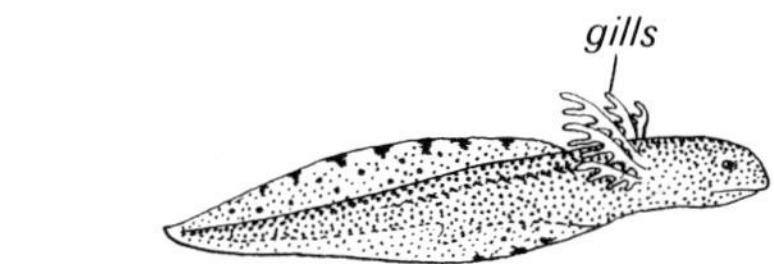

turn to pages 25, 26, 27

---

3. If the animal has a sucker at each end of its body, it is a LEECH.

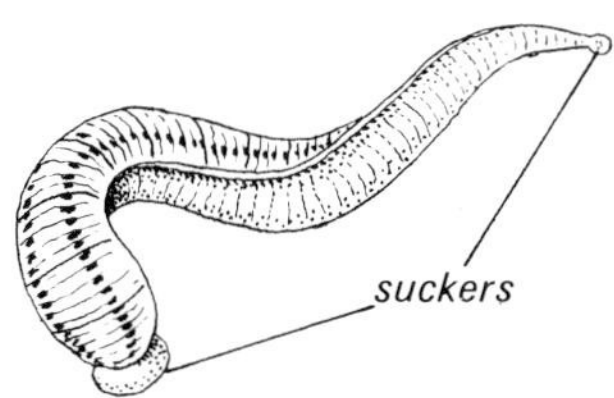

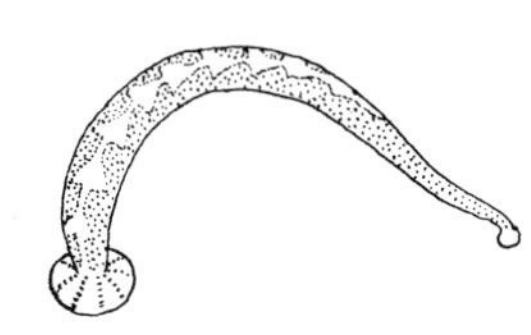

turn to pages 46, 47

---

4. If the animal looks like this, it is a RAT-TAILED MAGGOT, the LARVA of a DRONEFLY.

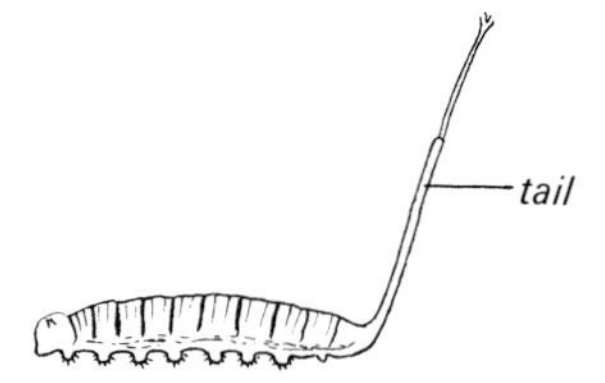

turn to page 42

---

5. If the animal has a smooth, flattened body, and glides over hard surfaces, it is a FLATWORM.

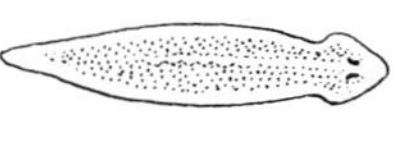

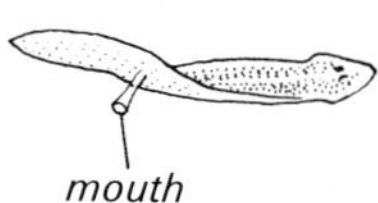

turn to page 47

From page 8, clue 10

1. If the animal has a body made up of rings (segments) with groups of bristles at its head or tail end, and has jerky, wriggling movements it may be a GNAT or MIDGE LARVA. If the animal looks like this but does not move jerkily, it is probably a BLACKFLY LARVA.

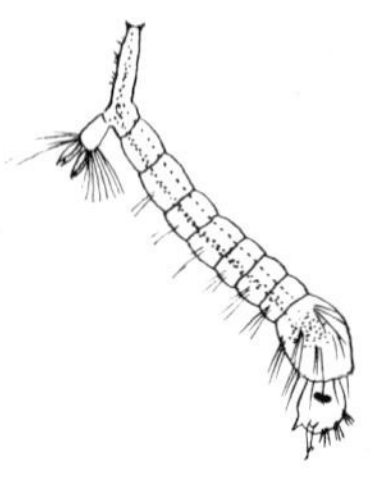

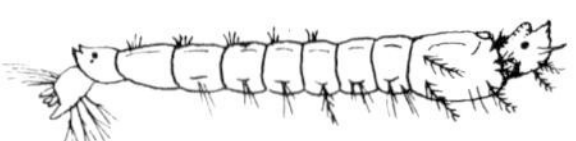

turn to pages 40, 41

---

2. If the animal has a large head and looks like this, it is a GNAT or MIDGE PUPA.

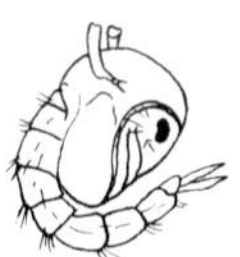

turn to pages 40, 41

---

3. If the animal has a body made up of rings (segments) with very short bristles on each ring, it is a WORM.

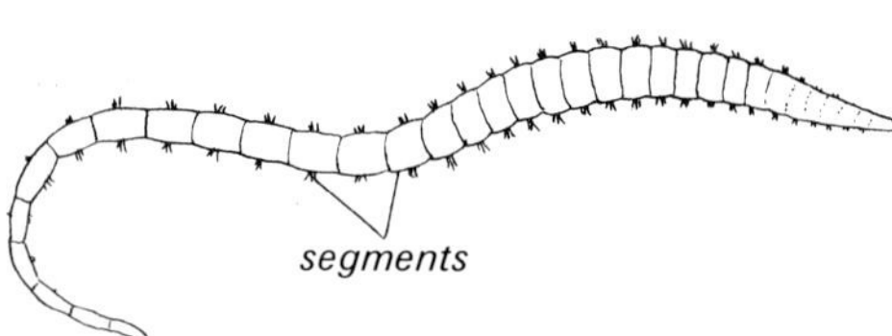

turn to pages 46, 47

From page 8, clue 10

4. If the animal has tentacles on one end of its body, it is HYDRA.

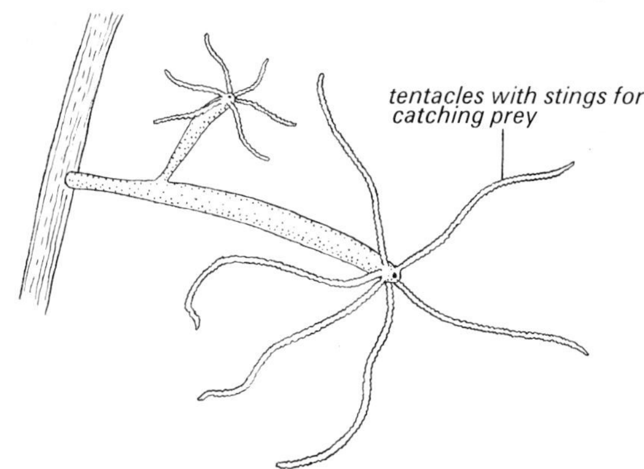

turn to page 47

---

5. If the animal is minute and looks like this, it may be a WHEEL-ANIMAL or ROTIFER.

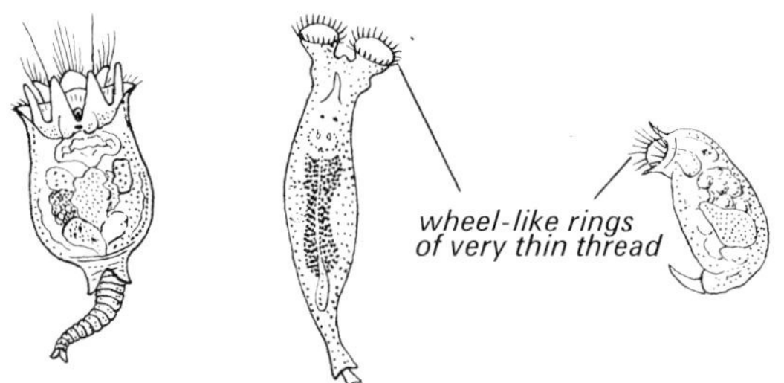

turn to page 47

---

6. If the animals are minute and colourless, they belong to a group of very simple animals called PROTOZOA.

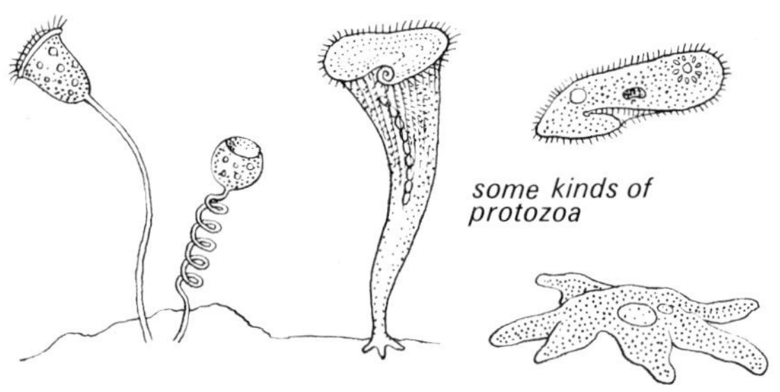

If you want to know more about these animals you will need to look at other books (see page 60).

---

7. If it does not look like any of these it may be EGGS.

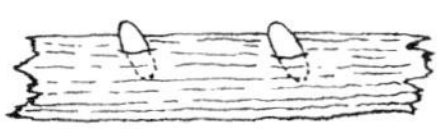

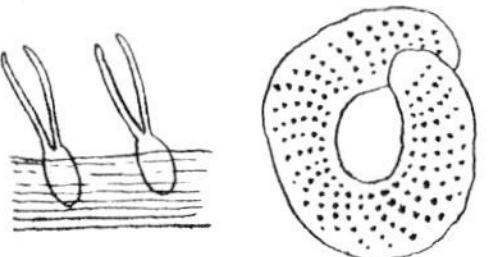

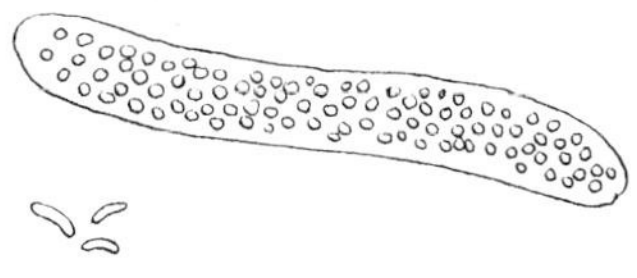

turn to pages 22, 23

From page 17, clue 1

1. If the animal has one shell — go on to clue 3
   If the animal has two shells — go on to clue 2

---

2. If the shells are large, dark, and look like this, it is a FRESHWATER MUSSEL.

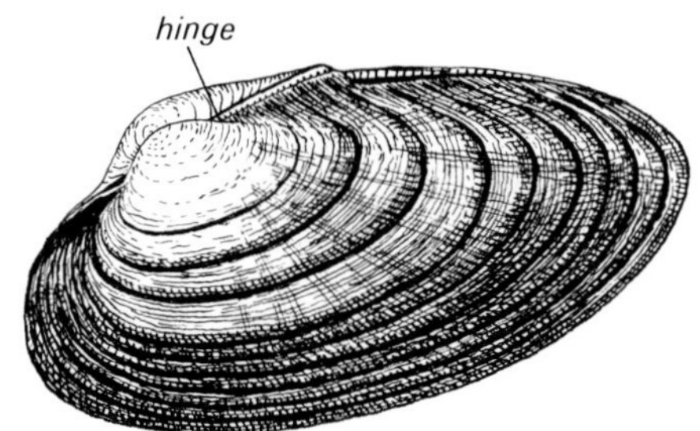

turn to pages 49, 50

If the shells are small, pale, and look like this, it is a PEA or ORB COCKLE.

turn to pages 49, 50

---

3. If the shell is a flat coil, it is a RAMSHORN SNAIL.

turn to pages 48, 49

If the shell is pointed

go on to clue 4, page 21

4. If the shell is brown with the opening to the right, and the tentacles are small with the eyes at the base, it is probably a POND SNAIL.

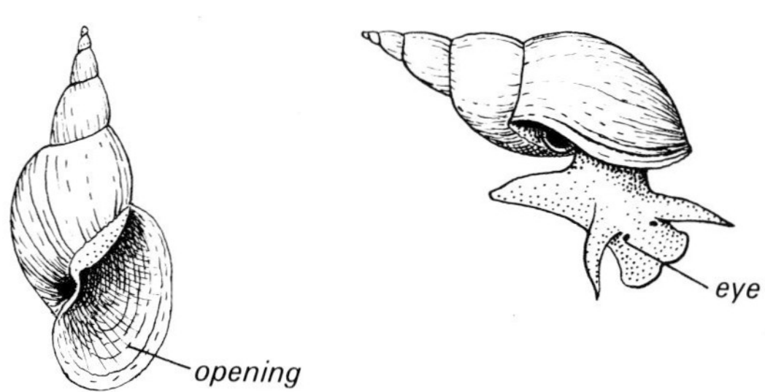

turn to pages 48, 49

If it looks like this, has an opening to the left, and is very shiny, it is probably a BLADDER SNAIL.

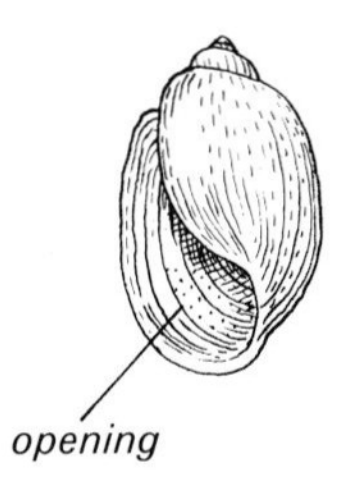

turn to pages 48, 49

If there is a shell-like plate (operculum) on its foot, it is a FRESHWATER WINKLE or VALVE SNAIL.

turn to pages 48, 49

EGGS from page 19, clue 7

If you look at the eggs of many freshwater animals under magnification you will be able to see, inside the eggs, animals at different stages of development (see page 24). If you find eggs like the ones illustrated on these pages turn to the page number by the drawing.

Eggs surrounded by jelly, floating on water

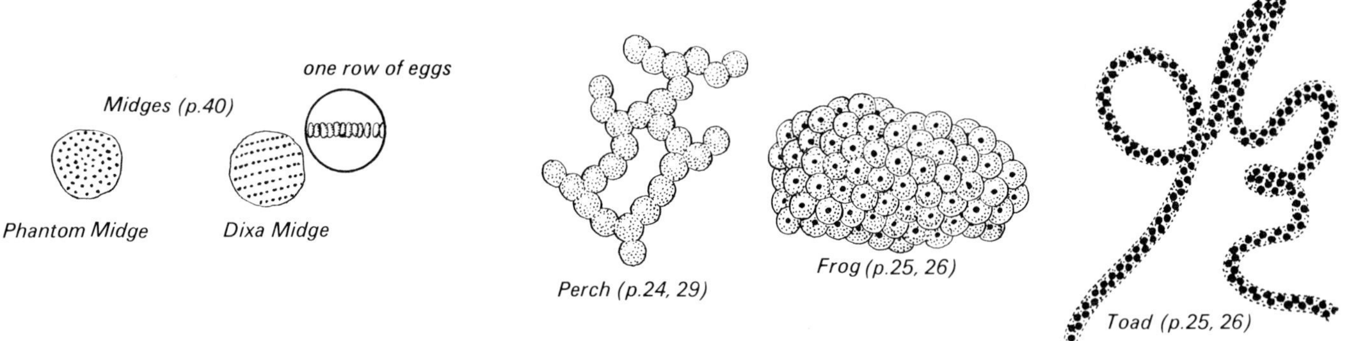

Eggs surrounded by jelly attached to plants and stones

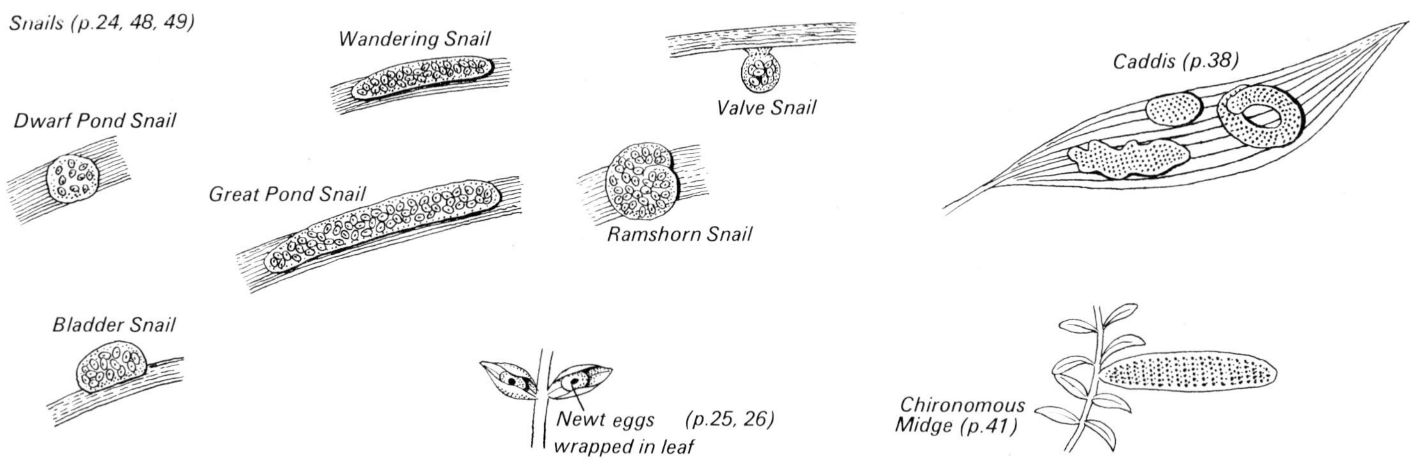

Eggs floating on water

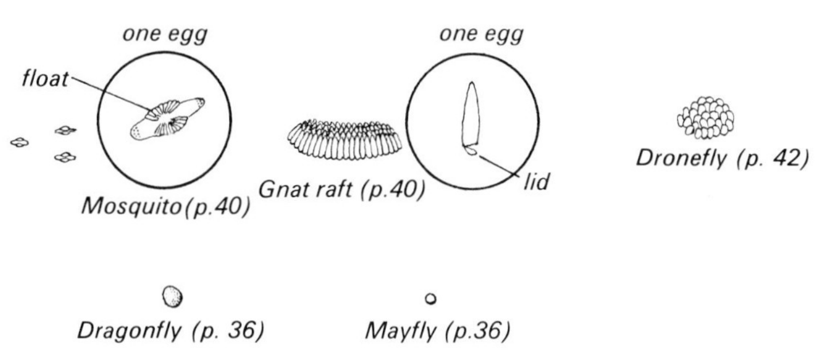

Eggs laid inside plant stems

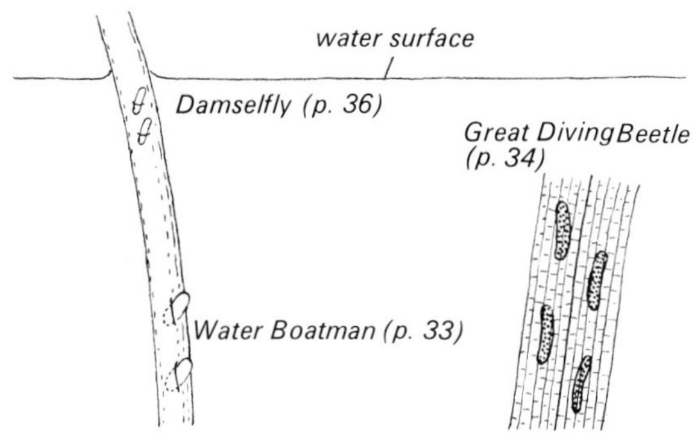

Eggs laid at the bottom of a pond or stream

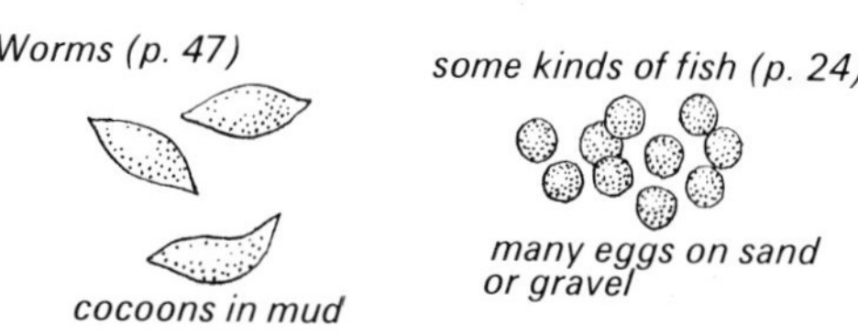

Eggs laid on plants above the water

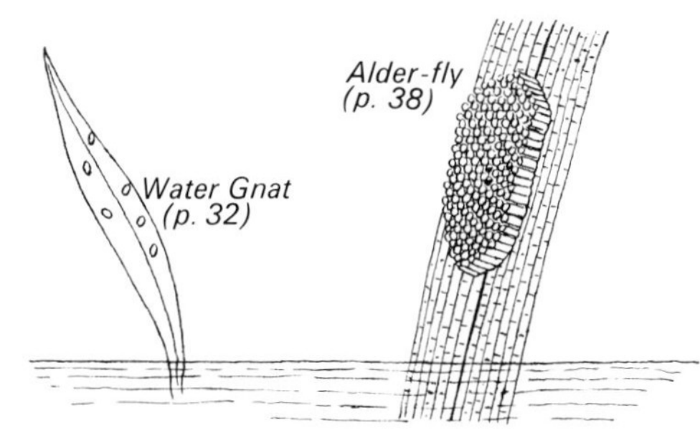

Eggs laid on plant stems or stones in the water

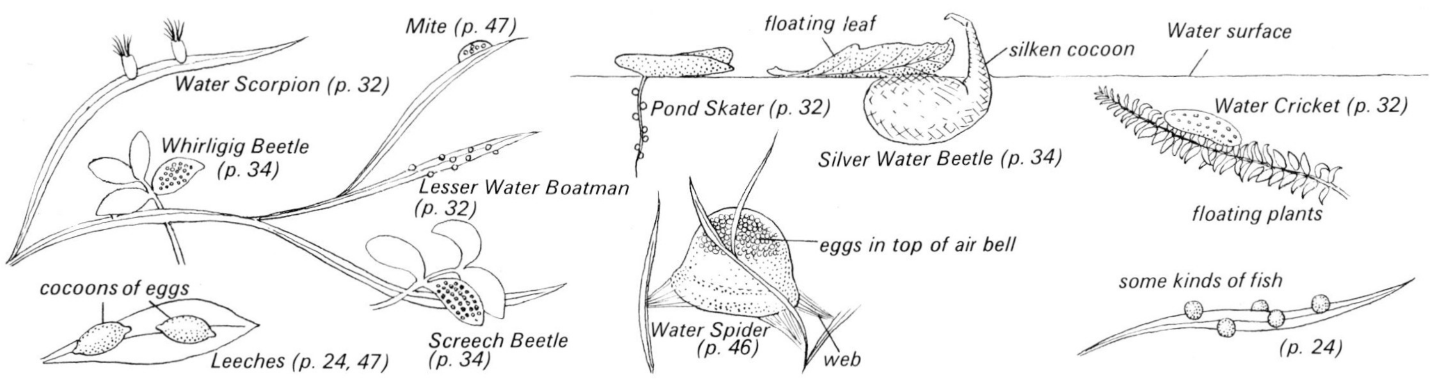

If you find eggs and wish to watch them develop, keep them in a shallow dish of water.

LEECH

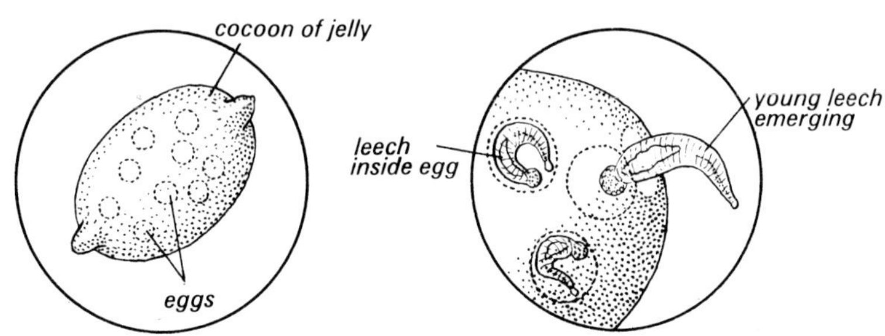

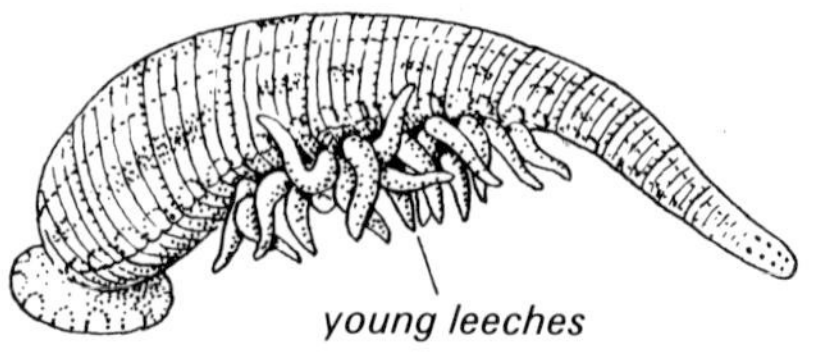

Some snail leeches brood their eggs, the young cling to the adult when they hatch.

FISH

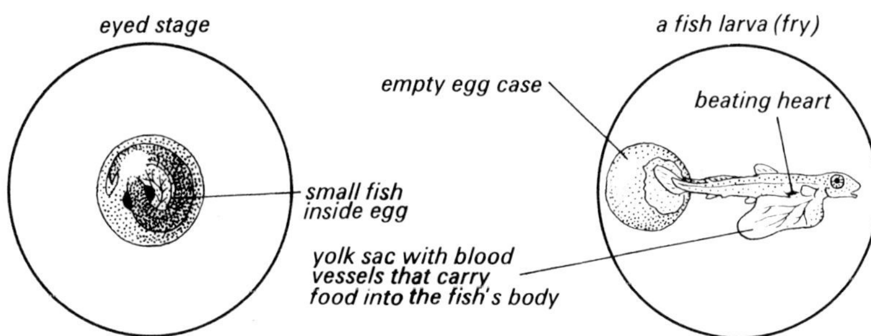

Some kinds of fish use up all the yolk before they hatch. Young fish, called parr, begin to show colour and fins more like their parents.

SNAILS

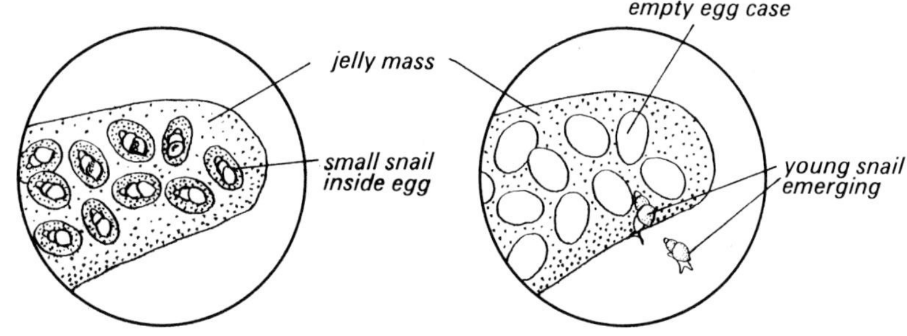

As the snail grows, the mantle makes new shell (see page 48).

Freshwater winkle eggs hatch inside the winkle's body; the young winkles emerge from a hole near the head.

FROG and TOAD

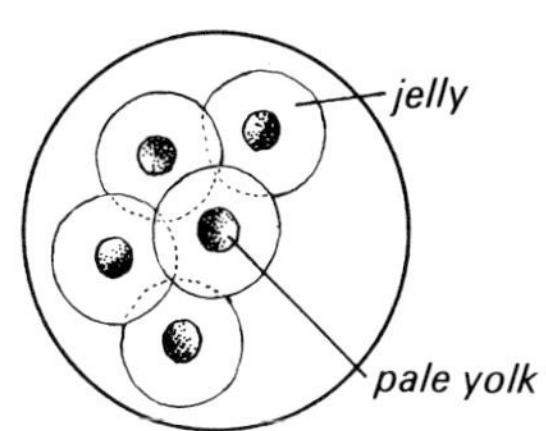

1. Eggs (March–April).

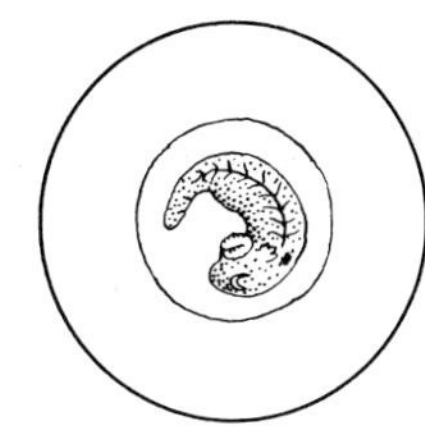

2. Tadpole formed inside egg.

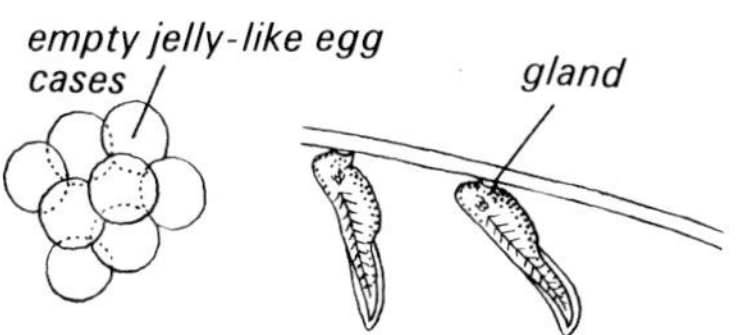

3. Newly hatched tadpoles are attached to plants by sticky slime from a gland.

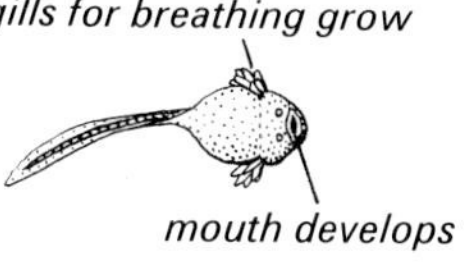

4. Tadpoles swim freely and feed by sucking decaying leaves and stems.

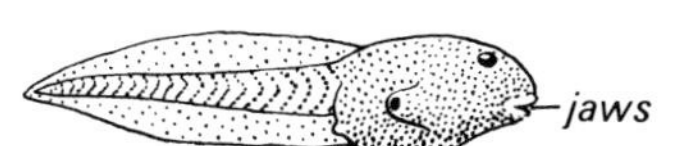

5. Jaws with horny teeth grow and the tadpole begins to eat small animals as well as plants. A flap of skin grows back over the gills.

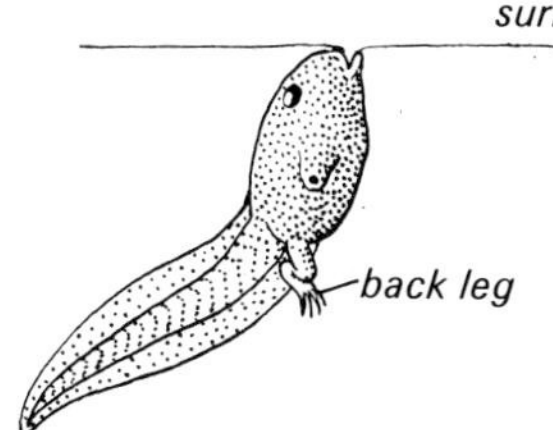

6. Back legs begin to grow.

7. Front legs appear.

Tadpoles come to the surface to breathe air through their mouths when their lungs grow.

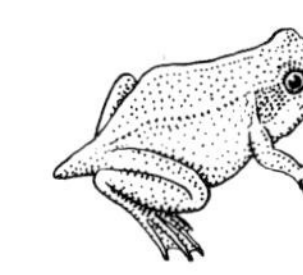

8. Tail disappears and the small frog leaves the water (June–July).

NEWT

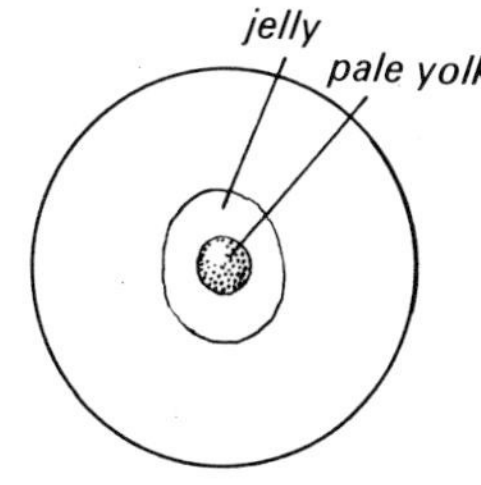

1. Egg.

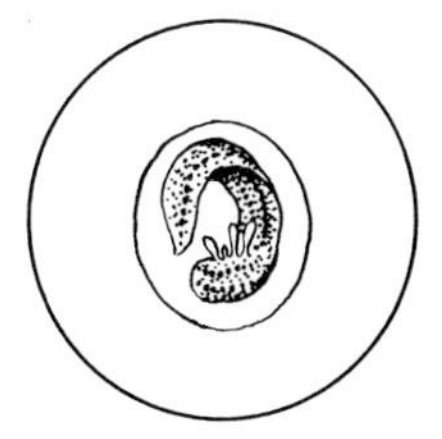

2. Tadpole formed inside egg.

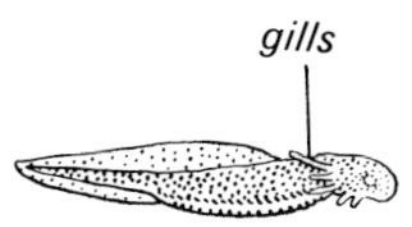

3. Gills for breathing grow.

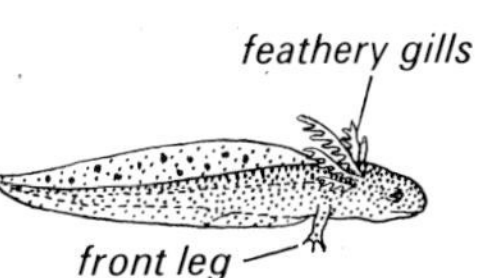

4. Front legs grow.

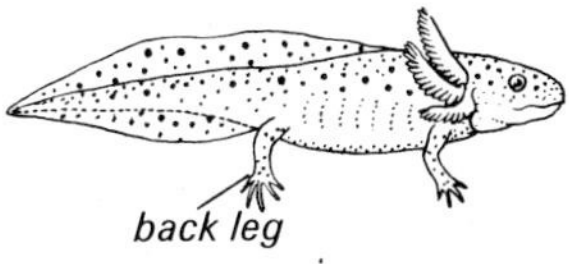

5. Back legs grow.

When the gills have been replaced by lungs the young newts leave the water (mid August).

Newt tadpoles feed on waterfleas and very small worms.

 From page 6, clue 1

AMPHIBIANS

Frogs, toads, and newts are always found in damp places. They often hide in holes or under stones in the daytime and move about at night. In spring they return to the water for a short time to mate and lay eggs (for tadpoles see page 25). Adults breathe through their moist skin, and also gulp air through their mouths. Watch the movements of their throats as they push the air into their lungs.

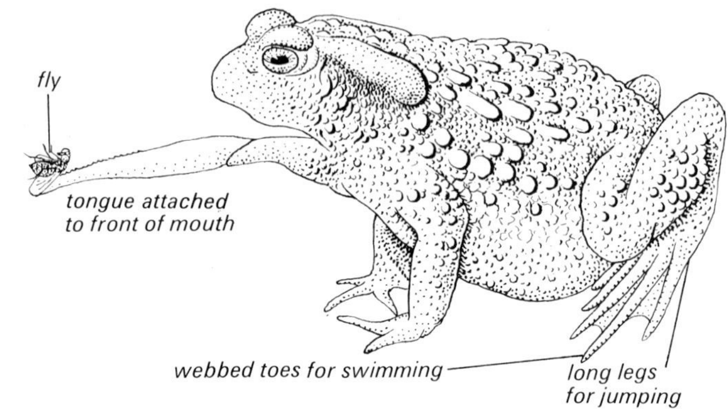

Amphibians are carnivorous (see page 53). They catch flies, small worms, and other small animals by flicking out their long tongues.

Amphibians sometimes shed their skins (see page 51).

A frog's colouring becomes light or dark to match its surroundings. To watch this, find two frogs of the same shade. Put one into a dark bowl and one into a light bowl. After ten minutes compare their colour by putting them together again. You can also find out how long it takes them to look the same colour again.

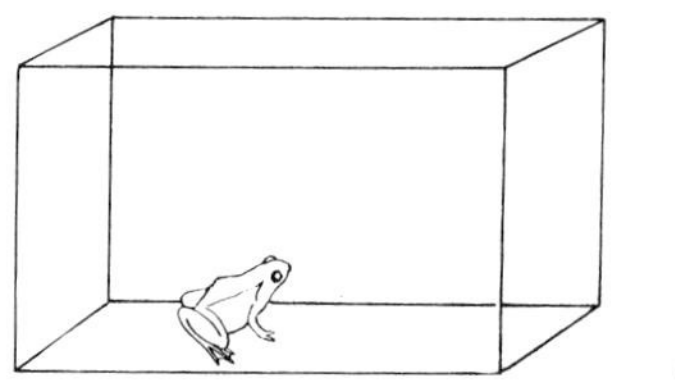

The male frog has a large thumb pad on his front leg which helps him to cling to the female's back while fertilizing the eggs she lays.

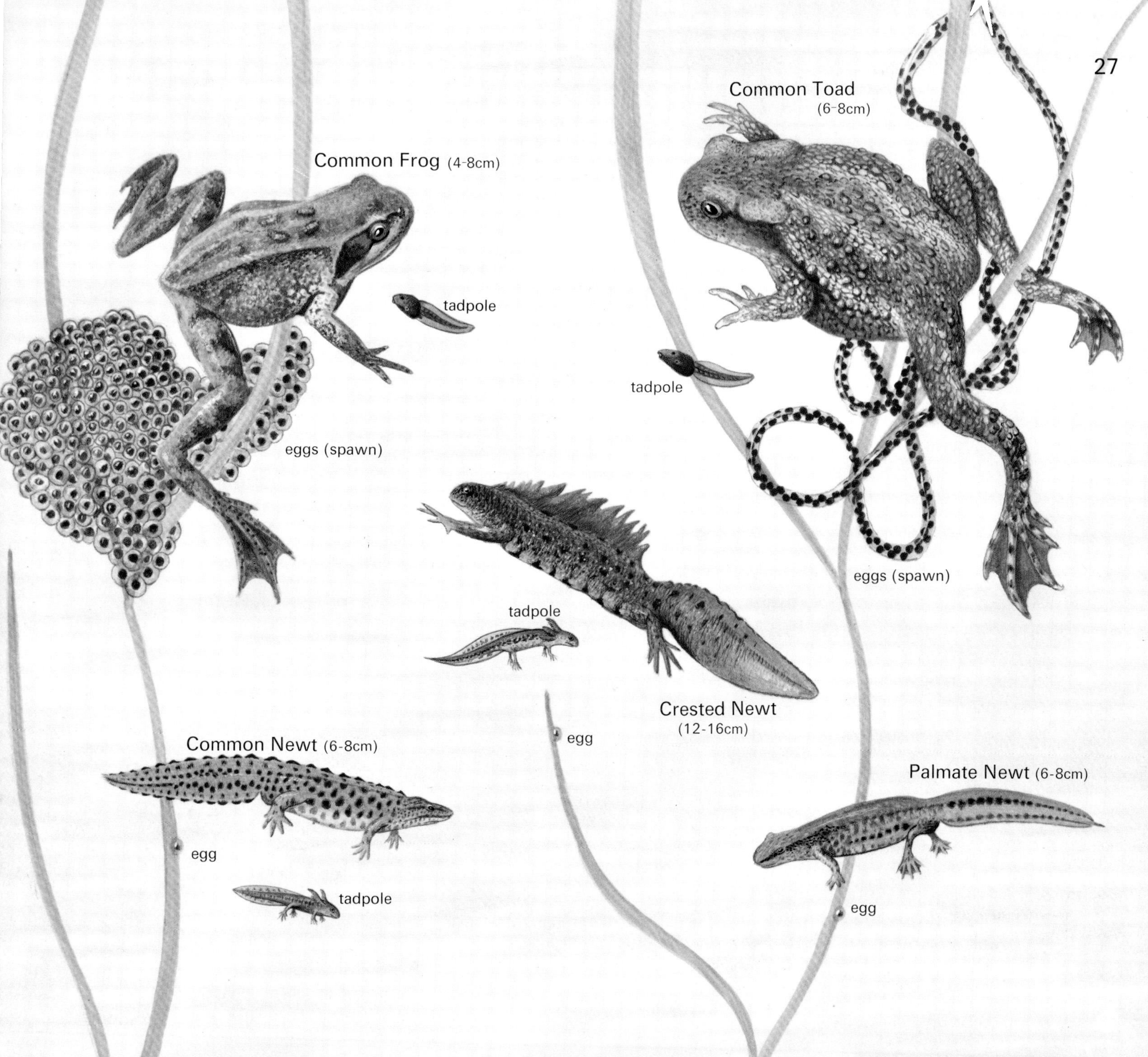
Common Toad
(6-8cm)
Common Frog (4-8cm)
tadpole
tadpole
eggs (spawn)
eggs (spawn)
tadpole
Crested Newt
(12-16cm)
egg
Common Newt (6-8cm)
Palmate Newt (6-8cm)
egg
tadpole
egg

FISH

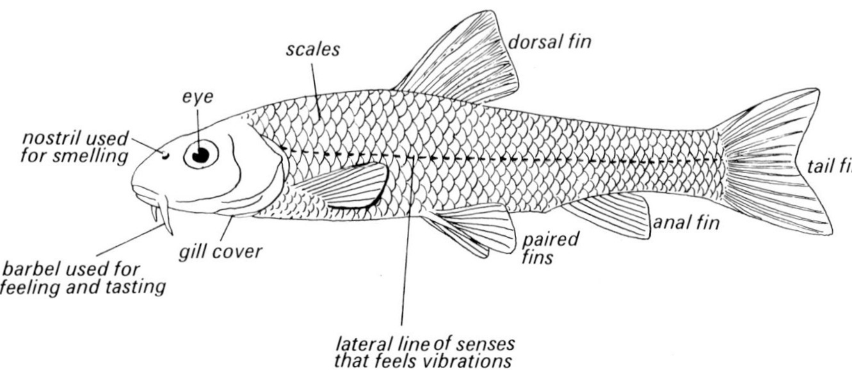

scale (enlarged)

part of scale outside the flesh

3rd winter

2nd winter

1st winter

growth rings are far apart in summer

in winter growth rings are close together showing very little growth

Fish have scales in their skin. The number of rings on a scale gives the approximate age of the fish. They can be counted if looked at under good magnification.

All fish bolt their food without chewing it. Carnivorous fish (see page 53) have large jaws with several rows of backward pointing teeth with which they catch their prey. These teeth are renewed when they wear out.

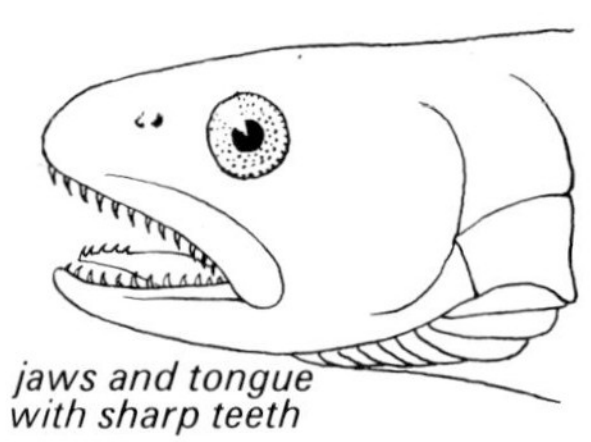

jaws and tongue with sharp teeth

The members of the CARP family (page 31) most often eat plants, but they also eat insect larvae and other small animals. These fish have small mouths without teeth on the jaws. Teeth in their throats begin to break up the food as they swallow it.

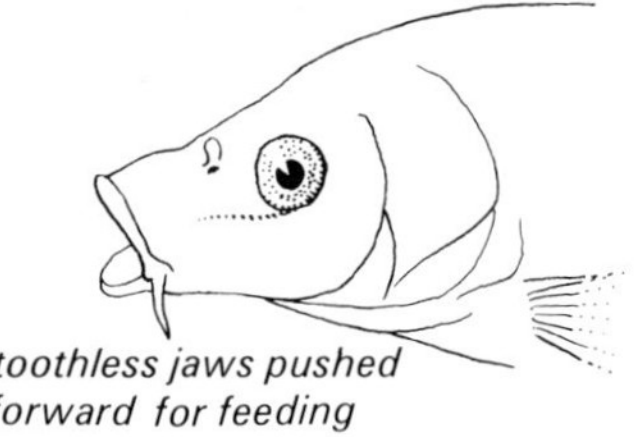

toothless jaws pushed forward for feeding

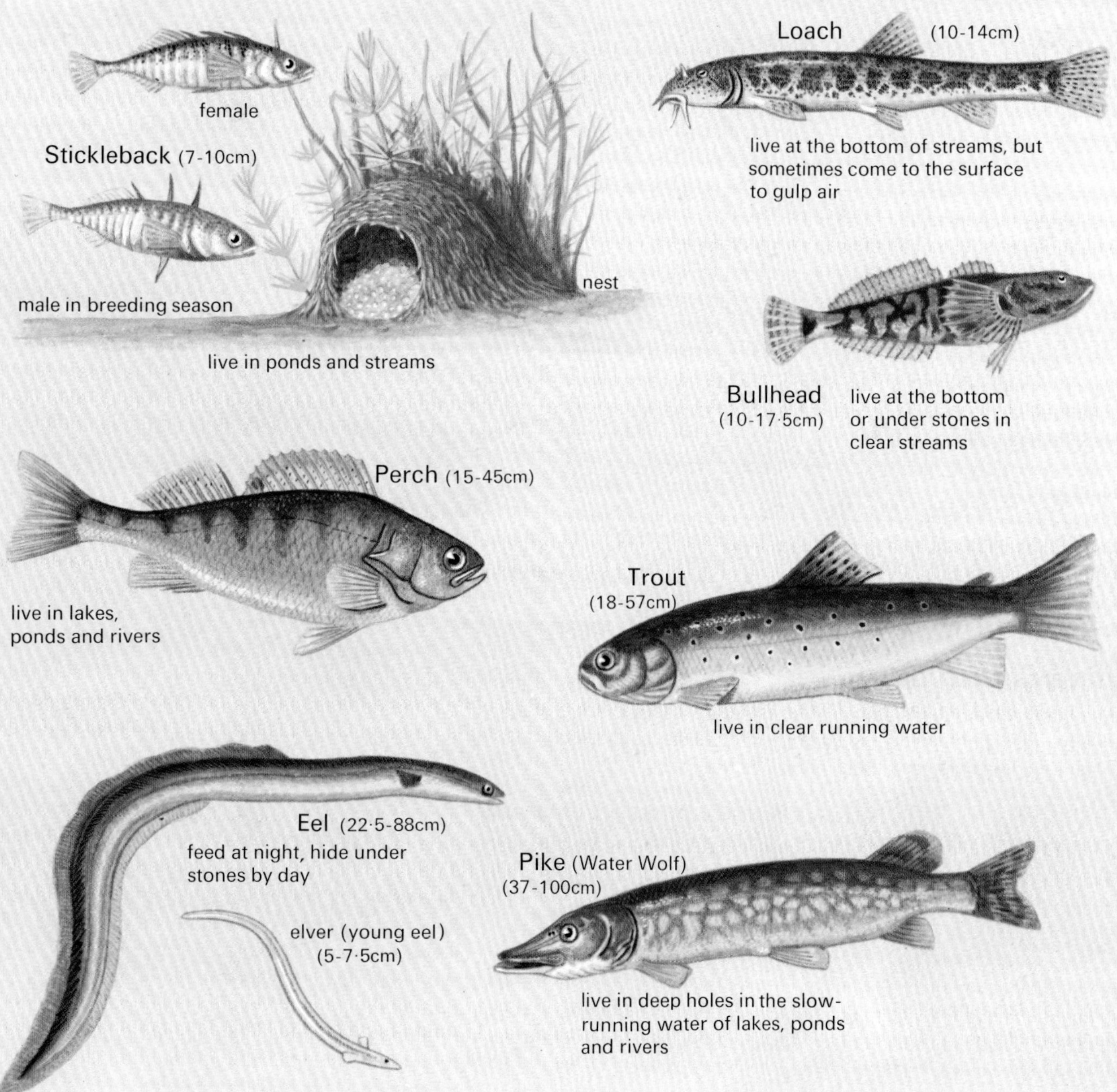
female
Stickleback (7-10cm)
male in breeding season
nest
live in ponds and streams
Loach (10-14cm)
live at the bottom of streams, but sometimes come to the surface to gulp air
Bullhead (10-17·5cm)
live at the bottom or under stones in clear streams
Perch (15-45cm)
live in lakes, ponds and rivers
Trout (18-57cm)
live in clear running water
Eel (22·5-88cm)
feed at night, hide under stones by day
elver (young eel) (5-7·5cm)
Pike (Water Wolf) (37-100cm)
live in deep holes in the slow-running water of lakes, ponds and rivers

FISH

From pages 9, 10, 11

Fish breathe by taking oxygen from the water. As a fish opens and closes its mouth it takes in water, but instead of swallowing it, it pushes it over the gills and out under the gill covers (see page 56).

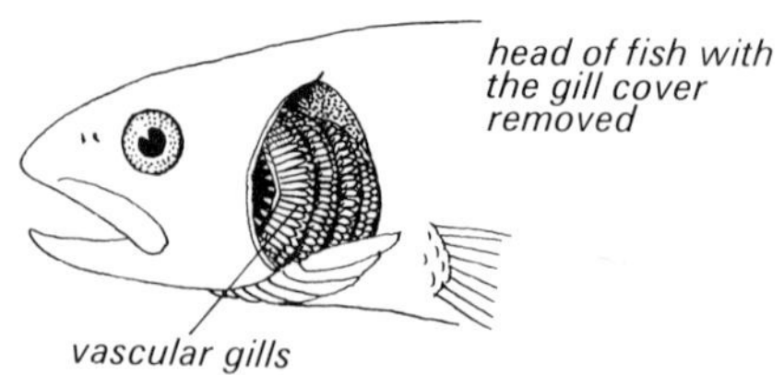

Most fish can move easily through water because they are streamlined. The curving movements that push the fish along are produced by the muscles (flesh) in the body and tail.

Body and tail fins help the fish to balance and change direction.

Carnivorous fish and the small fish on which they prey, live together in the same water.

Freshwater fish most often lay eggs on sand or gravel in still water. Male bullheads and sticklebacks make nests in which the females lay eggs. The eggs are fertilized by sperm (milt) from the male after the female has laid them (see pages 5, 22, 24, 29).

nest of Stickleback

male Stickleback fanning with its fins to aerate the eggs

male guarding and aerating the eggs

stone

Bullhead eggs in hollow attached to a stone

Eels swim out to sea to lay their eggs and then die. The young, called elvers, swim back to the rivers in the spring (see page 29).

FISH THAT EAT PLANTS and SMALL ANIMALS

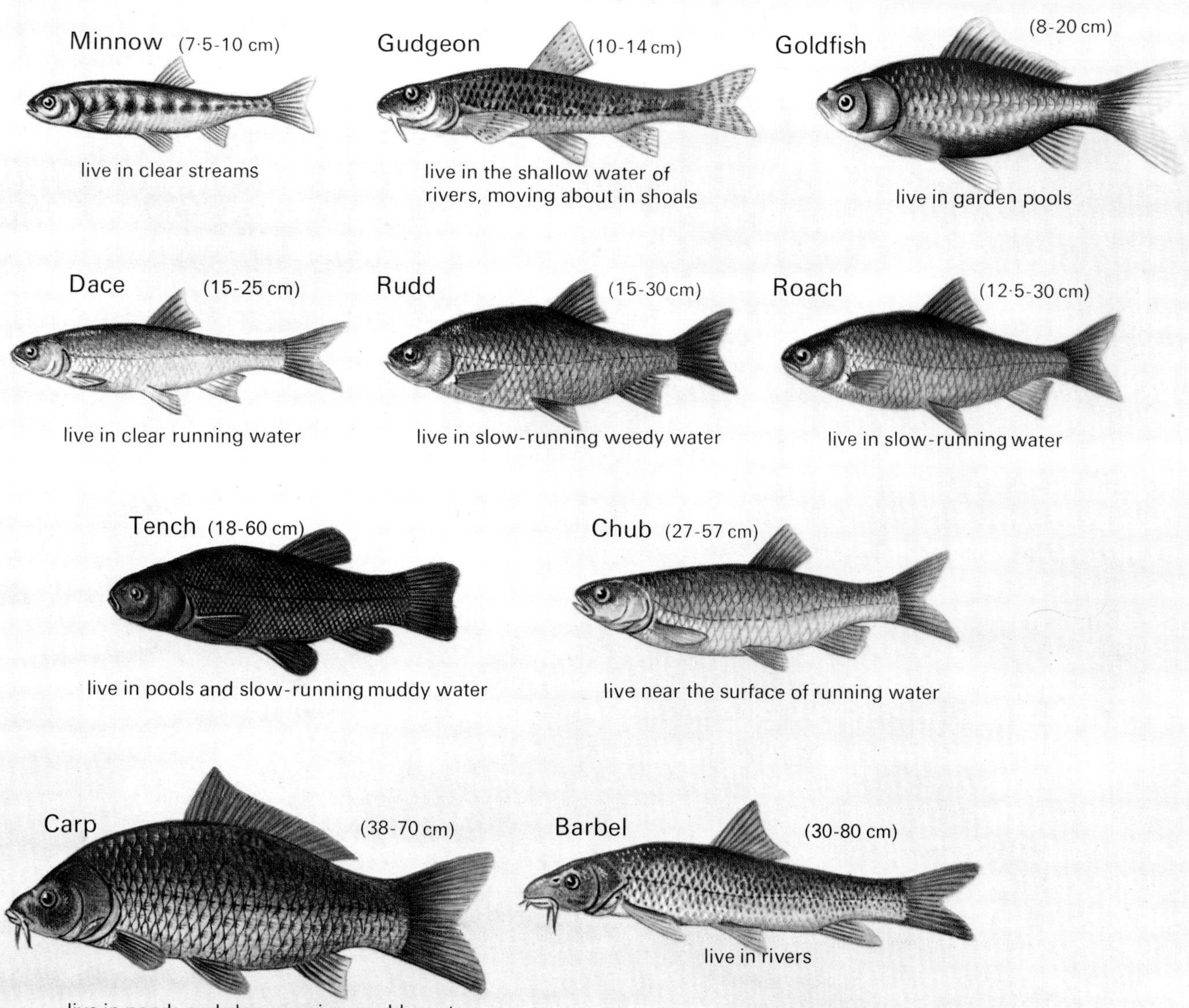

 From page 12, clue 1 and page 13, clues 5, 6

INSECTS—BUGS

Water bugs are most often found in the still water of ponds and the weedy edges of streams. They are carnivorous (see page 53) and have beak-like jaws for sucking juices from their prey.

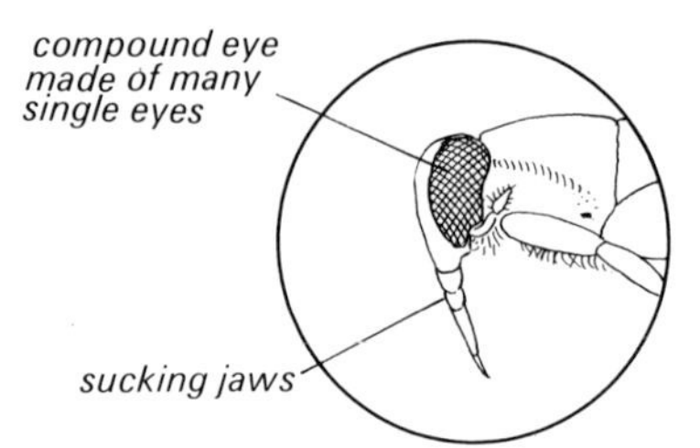

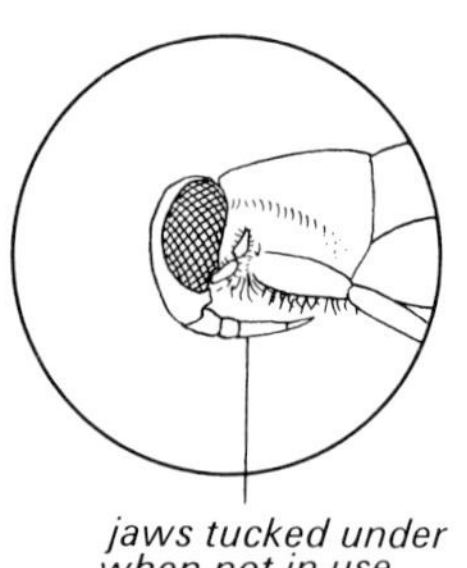

Water Boatmen breathe by coming to the surface of the water to collect a bubble of air over their hairy bodies and under their wings. They can stay down only by swimming hard or clinging to plants.

The Lesser Water Boatmen scavenge at the bottom of the water.

Water Boatmen may fly from pond to pond during the night.

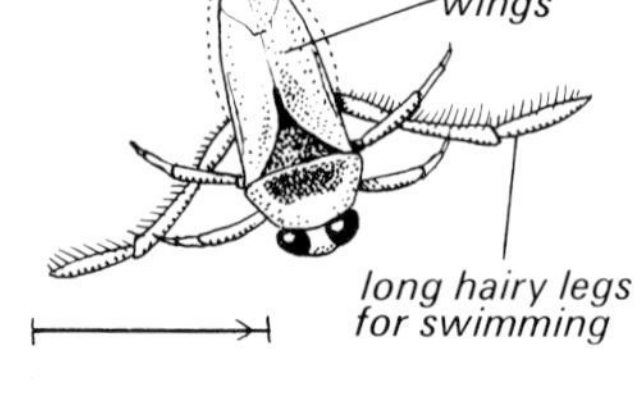

Water Scorpions are flat animals that live on the bottom at the edge of a pond. They do not fly.

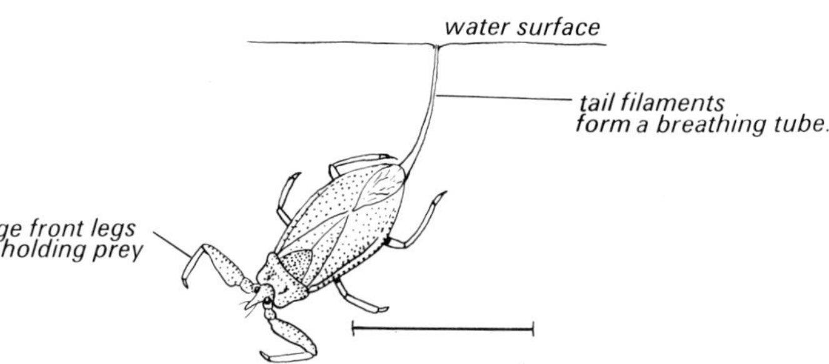

Pond Skaters, Water Gnats, and Water Crickets skim over the surface of the still water of ponds and the edges of streams. Water Gnats may also climb plants near the water.

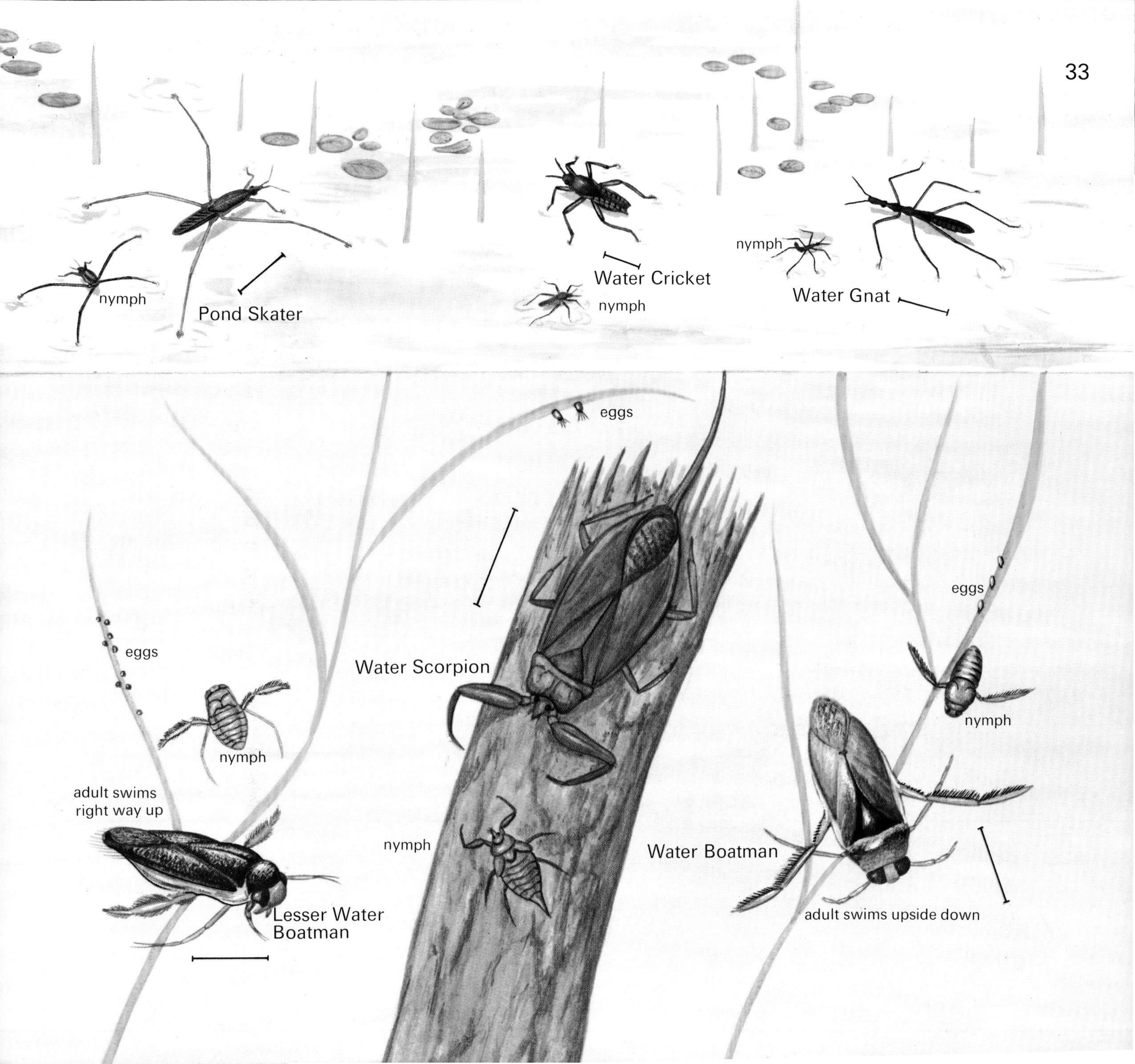

nymph
Pond Skater
Water Cricket
nymph
nymph
Water Gnat
eggs
eggs
eggs
Water Scorpion
nymph
nymph
adult swims right way up
nymph
Water Boatman
Lesser Water Boatman
adult swims upside down

 From page 12, clue 2 and page 14, clues 2, 3, 4

INSECTS
BEETLES

Water Beetles most often live in the still water of ponds and ditches. Most kinds of beetles and their larvae are carnivorous (see page 53); they have strong biting jaws for catching their prey (tadpoles and fish) and sucking the juices.

head of Great Diving Beetle
palps for smelling
slender antenna
biting jaws
compound eye made of many single eyes

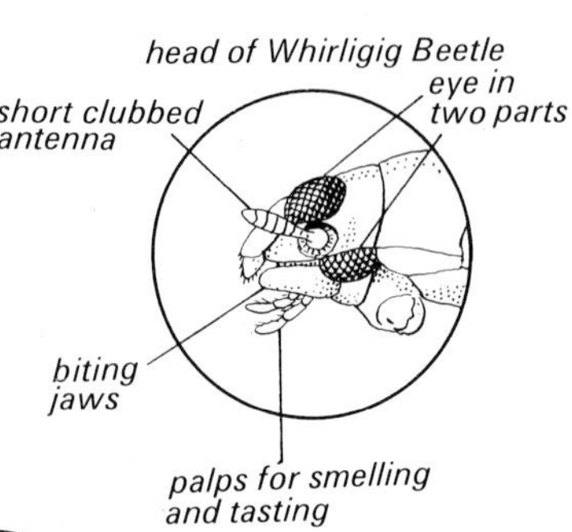

biting jaws
several single eyes
head of most beetle larvae

The Silver Water Beetle is herbivorous: its larvae eat snails.

head of Silver Water Beetle
long palps for smelling and touching
hairy clubbed antennae that help with breathing
compound eye made of many single eyes

Most beetles breathe by coming to the surface of the water to collect a bubble of air over their hairy bodies and under their wings (see page 56).

tip of abdomen breaks surface film to collect air
antenna breaks surface film to collect air
water surface
tail filaments break surface film to collect air (see p.57)
hairy legs aid swimming

Great Diving Beetle (3 cm)
Silver Water Beetle rising head first to the surface (3-4 cm)
larva of Water Beetle (4-6 cm)

Beetle larvae pupate in damp soil near the water (see pages 35, 54).

larva of Whirligig Beetle breathes in water
tracheal gills (see p.57)

The small black beetles that dart and whirl about on the surface are Whirligig Beetles. Screech beetles squeak when caught.

larva of Screech Beetle
tracheal gills (see p.57) for breathing in mud

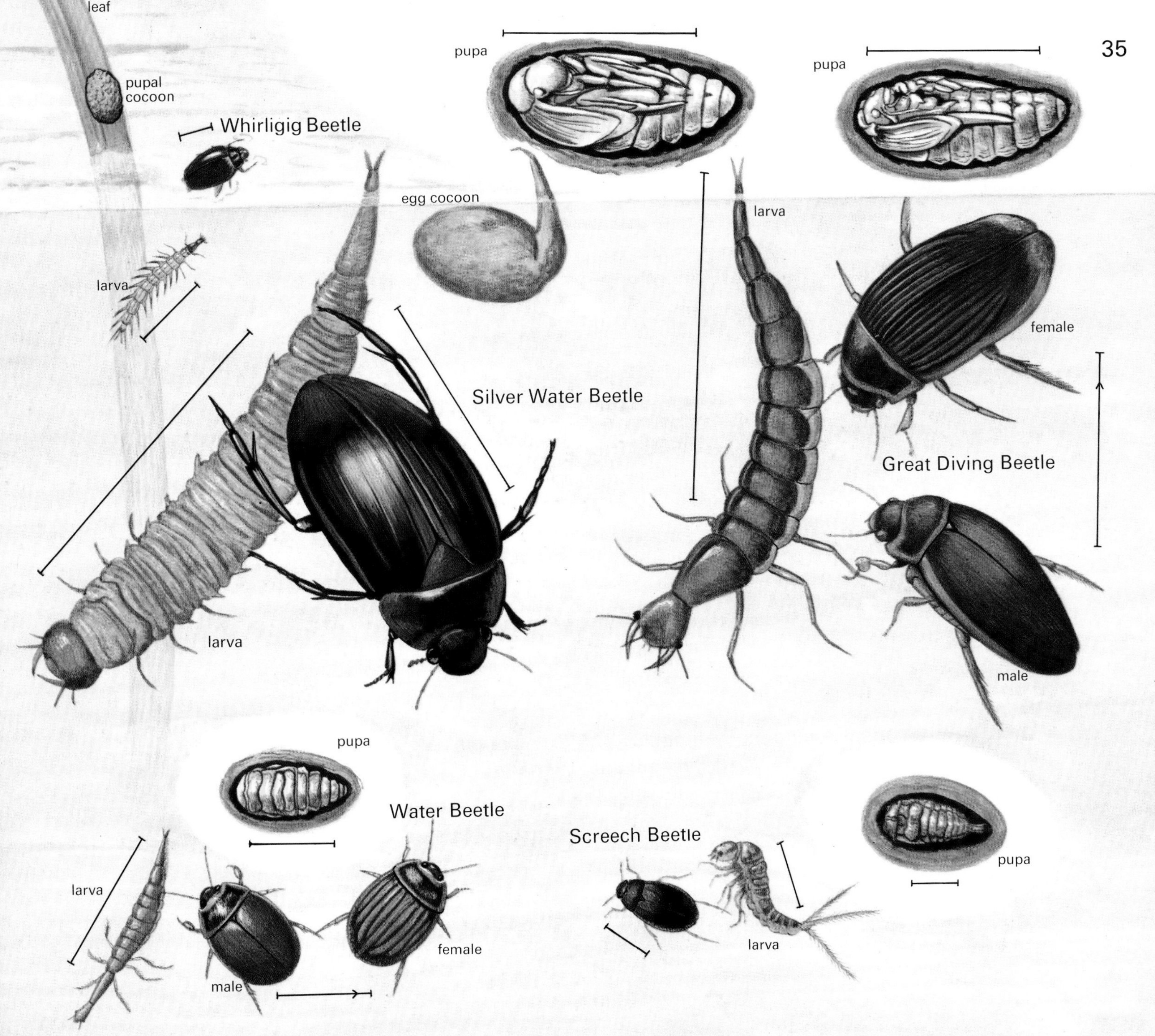
leaf
pupal cocoon
Whirligig Beetle
larva
pupa
egg cocoon
Silver Water Beetle
larva
pupa
larva
female
Great Diving Beetle
male
pupa
Water Beetle
larva
male
female
Screech Beetle
larva
pupa

From page 13, clue 2

INSECT NYMPHS

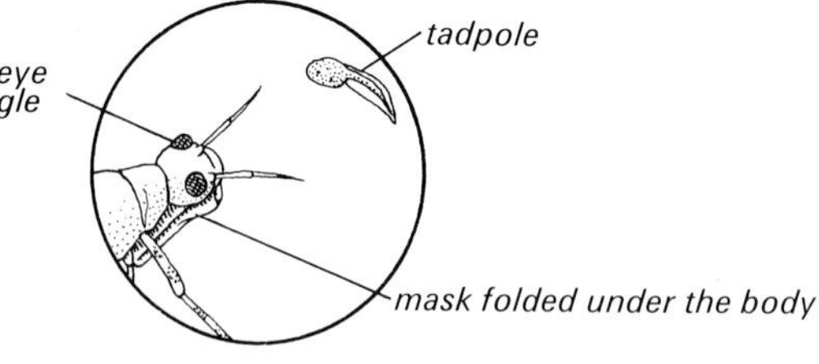

Damselfly nymph catching tadpole

For the adults of the insects on this page, which do not live in water, see the Clue Book of INSECTS, pages 32, 33.

DRAGONFLY AND DAMSELFLY NYMPHS

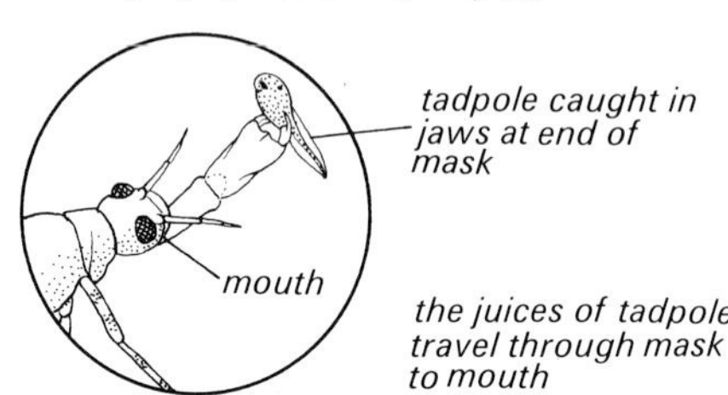

Dragonfly and Damselfly nymphs live among the weeds in still water. They are carnivorous (see page 53) and catch animals that come near them by the quick action of their jaws. They see animals coming with their large eyes.

When nymphs are full-grown (which may take two years) they climb out of the water and cling to the stems of plants. Then the last nymphal case bursts, and the adult emerges (see page 37). After mating the female drops the eggs singly into the water (see page 23).

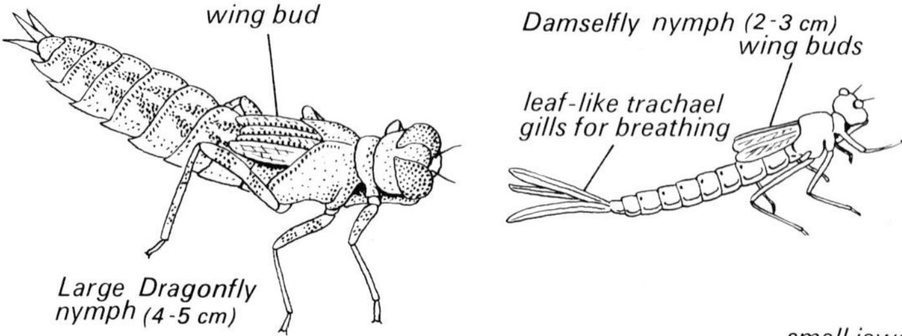

MAYFLY NYMPHS

Mayfly nymphs are scavengers (see page 53). They live at the bottom of the water. When the nymphs are nearly full-grown they climb out of the water and shed their skins twice before they become adult. After mating most females scatter eggs singly over the water.

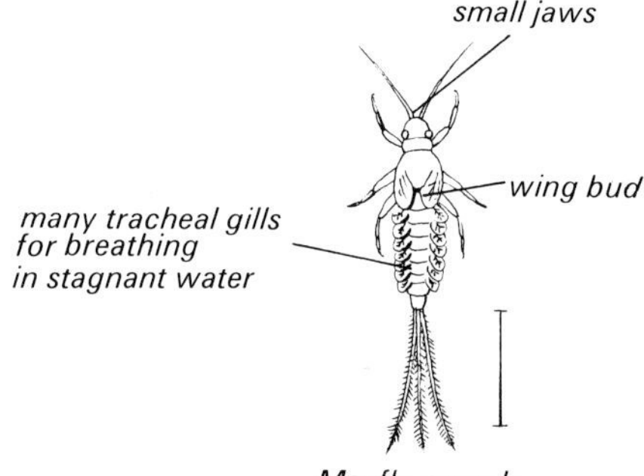

Mayfly nymph

Dragonfly, damselfly, and mayfly nymphs all breathe below water (see page 57). Sometimes large dragonfly nymphs move quickly by forcing a jet of water backwards out of their bodies.

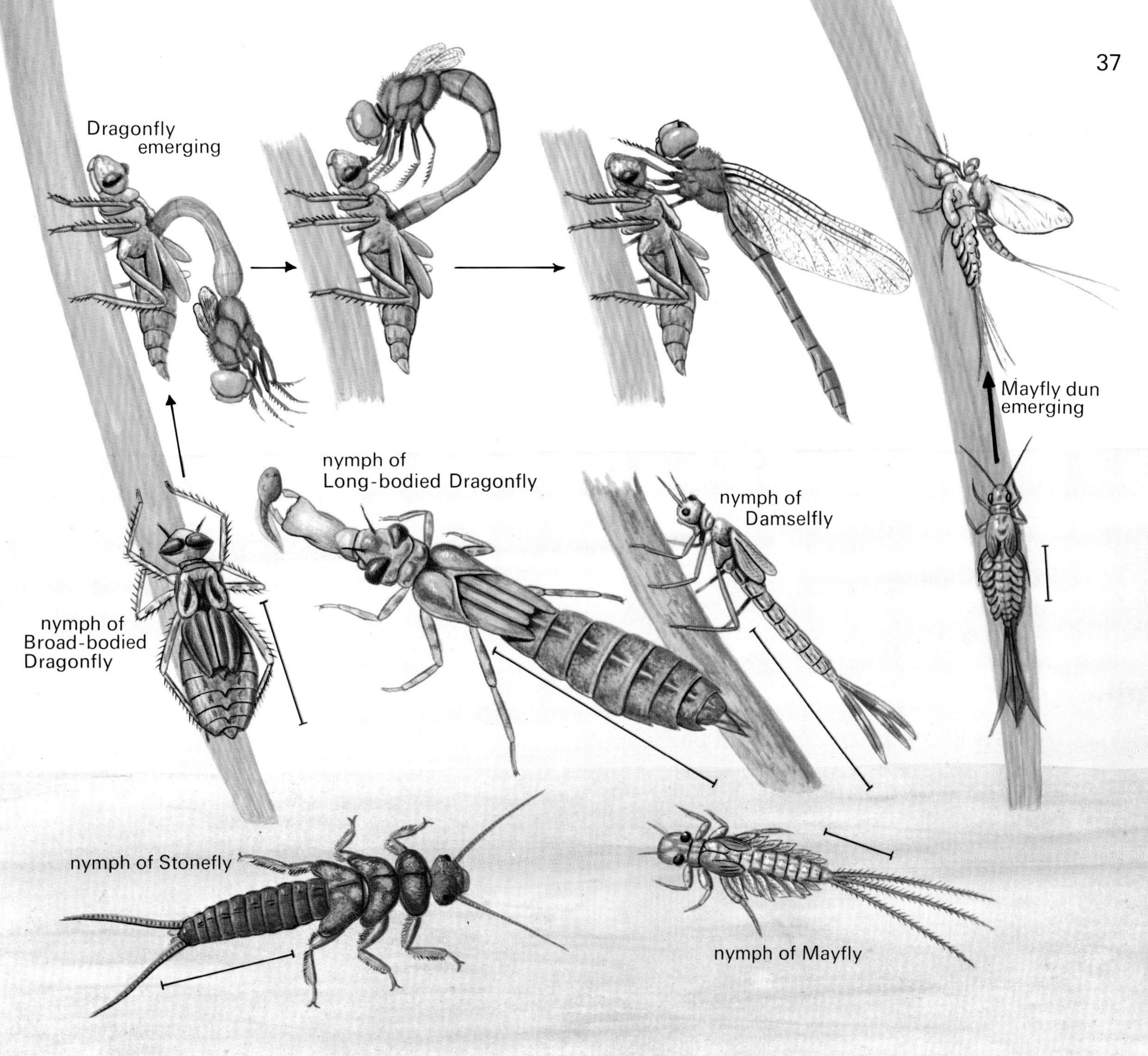
Dragonfly emerging
Mayfly dun emerging
nymph of Long-bodied Dragonfly
nymph of Damselfly
nymph of Broad-bodied Dragonfly
nymph of Stonefly
nymph of Mayfly

From page 14, clue 1 and page 15, clue 5

INSECT LARVAE and PUPAE

For the adults of the insects shown on this page, which do not live in water, see the Clue Book of INSECTS, pages 32, 33.

ALDER-FLY LARVAE

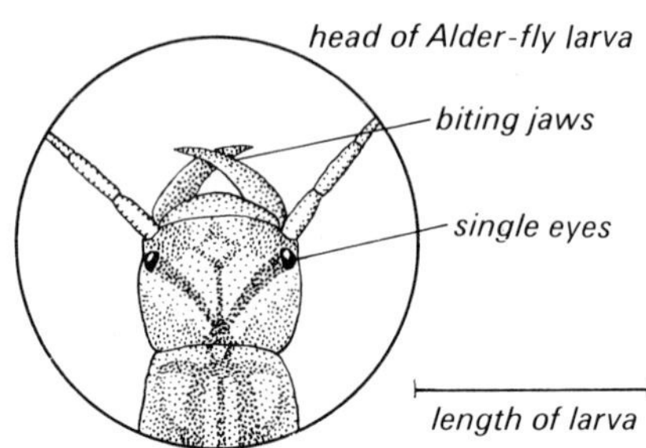

Alder-fly larvae are carnivorous (see page 53). They crawl about in the mud under water for nearly two years. When nearly full-grown the larvae crawl out of the water into damp earth to pupate (see page 4). After about three weeks the adult flies emerge and mate. The female lays clusters of eggs (see page 23).

CADDIS LARVAE and PUPAE

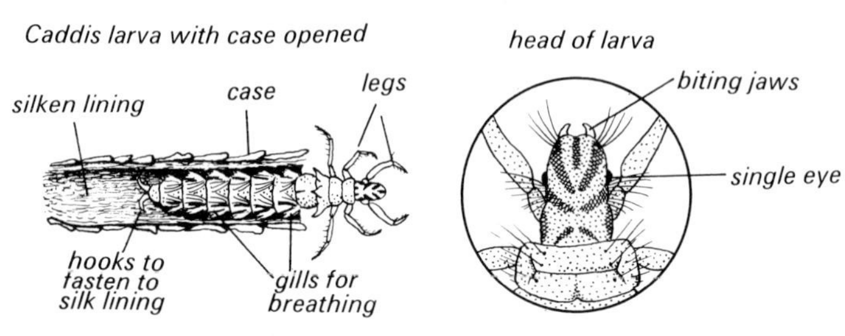

Caddis larvae most often live in still water, and crawl about on the bottom of ponds, lakes, and streams, carrying with them a case that covers the soft end of their bodies. Each kind of caddis larva uses a particular material to make its case (see page 39). Caddis larvae eat plants.

Caddis larvae spend the winter in water and pupate (see page 4) in their cases in early summer. The pupae cut their way out of the cases and climb out of the water before hatching into adult caddis flies; they mate, and the female lays a mass of eggs (see page 22).

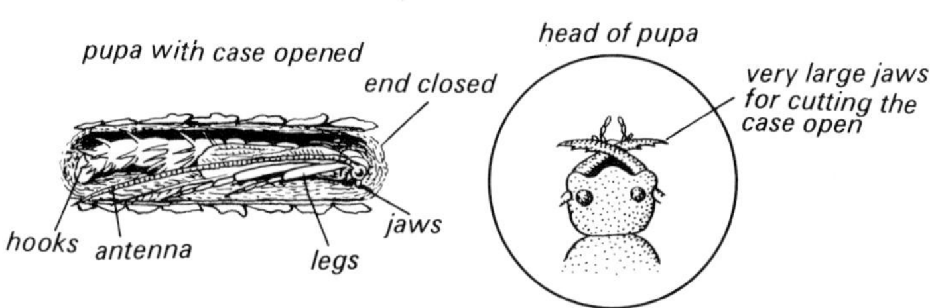

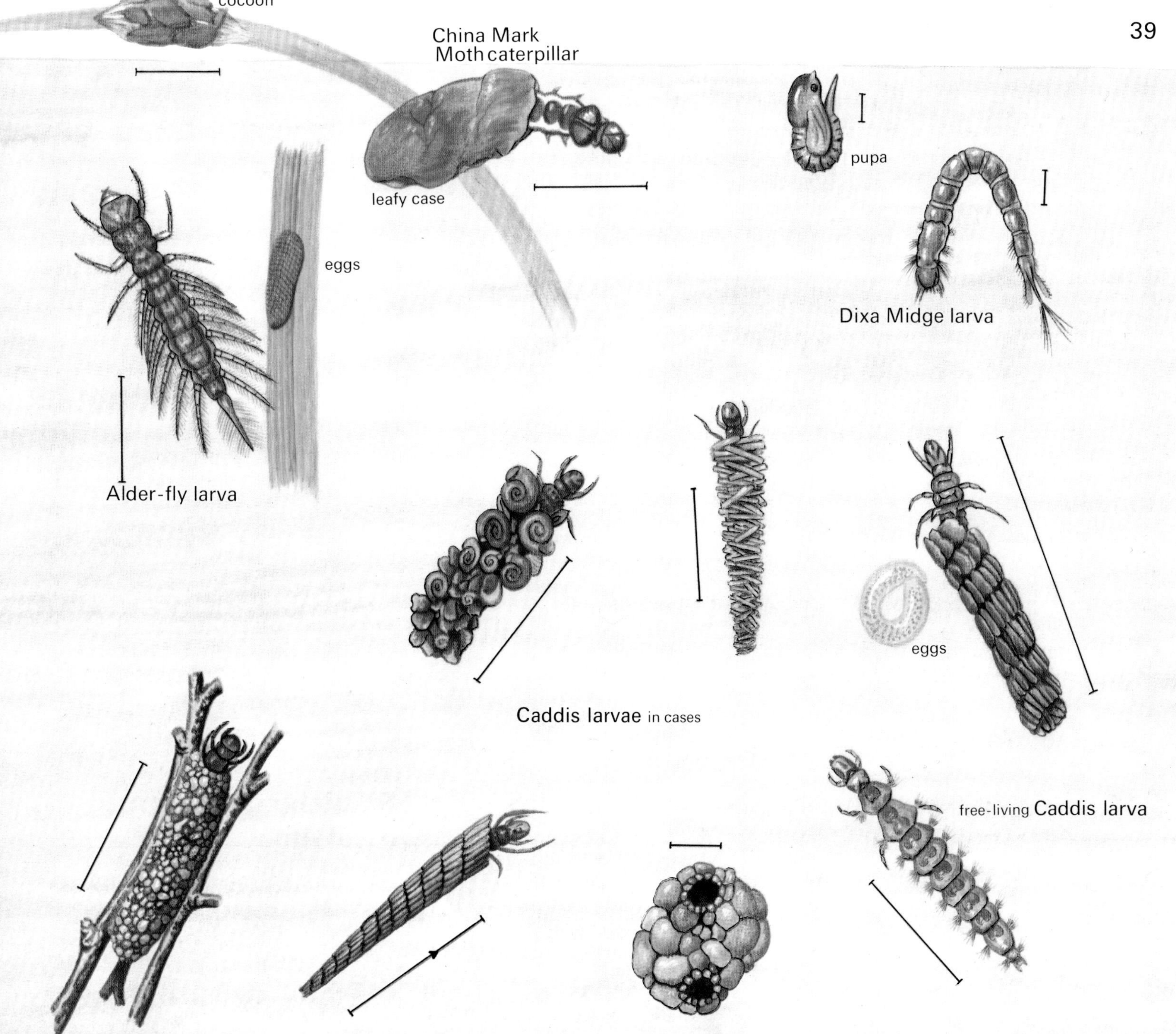
cocoon
China Mark
Moth caterpillar
leafy case
pupa
eggs
Dixa Midge larva
Alder-fly larva
eggs
Caddis larvae in cases
free-living Caddis larva

From page 18, clues 1, 2

INSECT LARVAE and PUPAE

For the adults of the insects shown on this page, which do not live in water, see the Clue Book of INSECTS, pages 42, 43.

Look carefully at the animal under good magnification.

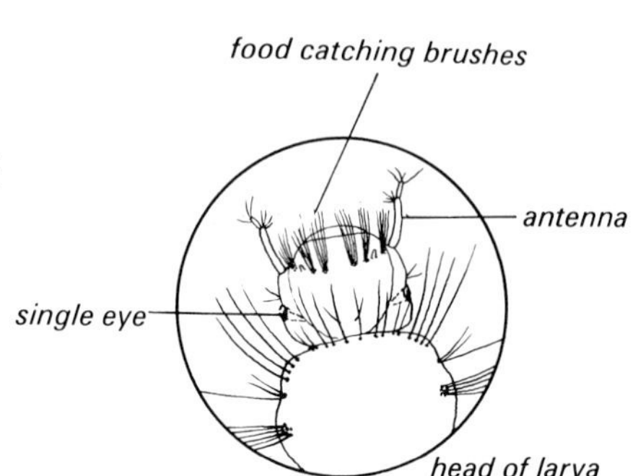

GNAT (sometimes called MOSQUITO) and MIDGE LARVAE live in still water, including water in rainwater butts and garden pools and move with quick, wriggling jerks. They are scavengers (see page 53) and feed by filtering food from the water through bristles on their heads.

Gnat larvae breathe through holes called SPIRACLES (see page 57), which collect air through the surface film of the water as they hang from it.

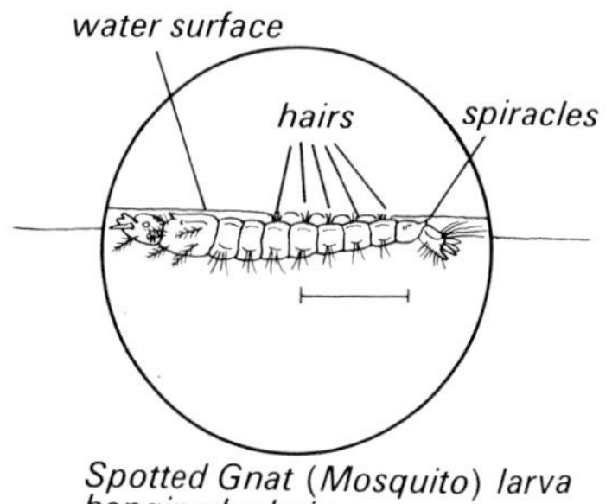

Spotted Gnat (Mosquito) larva hanging by hairs

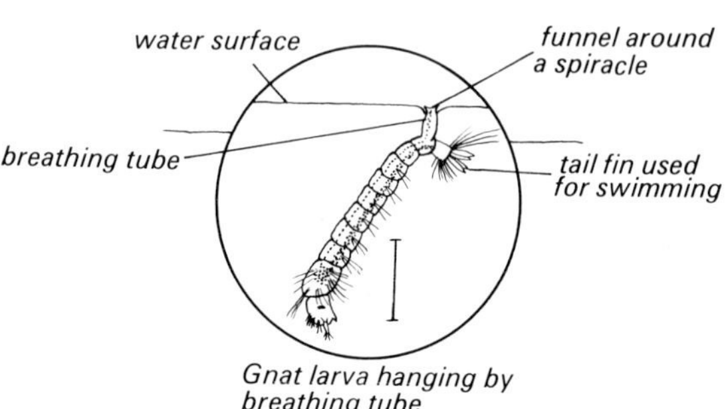

Gnat larva hanging by breathing tube

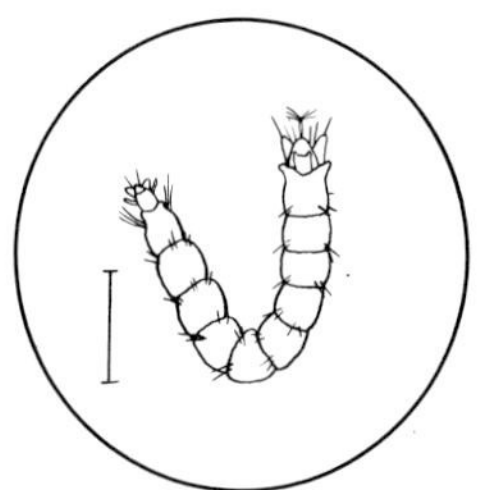

Dixa Midge larva, similar to Gnat larvae but U-shaped (see p.39)

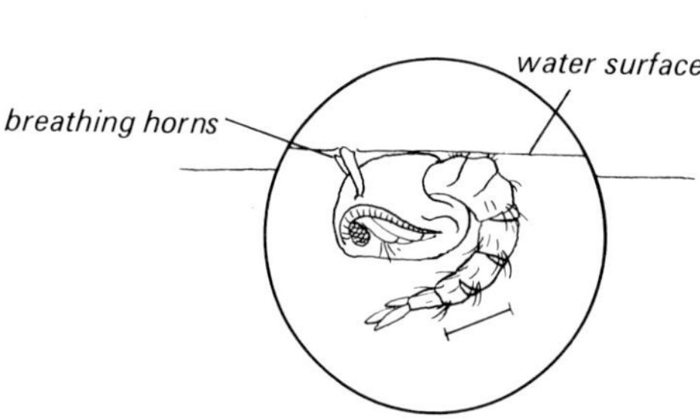

Spotted Gnat (Mosquito) pupa hanging by hairs

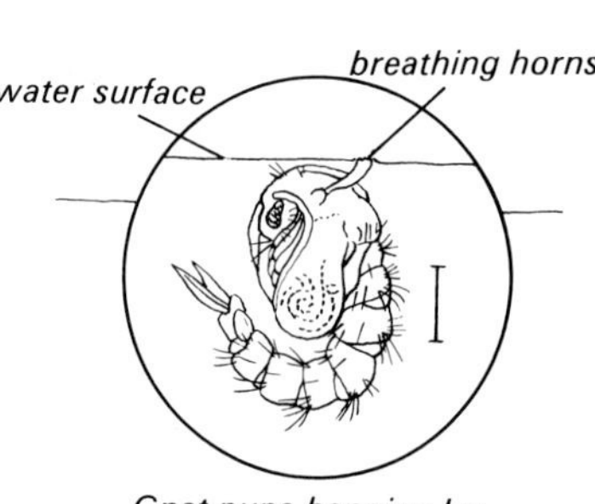

Gnat pupa hanging by breathing horns

CHIRONOMOUS LARVAE and PUPAE

Chironomous (Harlequin fly) larvae live in tubes in mud or on water plants; they sometimes leave their tubes and move jerkily in the water or scavenge (see page 53) for food in the mud.
Some larvae are called *Bloodworms* because they are red.

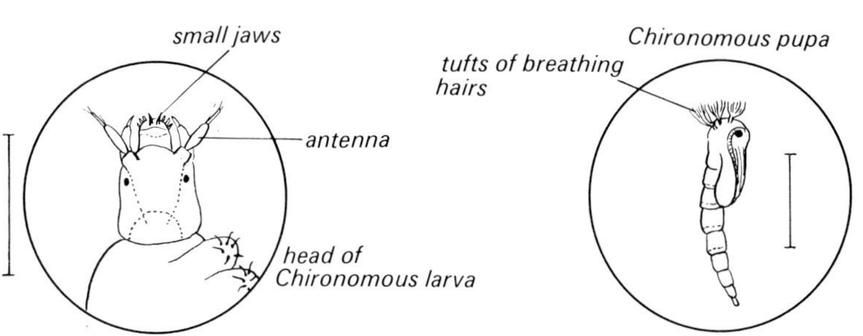

PHANTOM MIDGE LARVAE

Phantom midge larvae hang horizontally in the water. They are carnivorous (see page 53). They breathe through the skin all over their bodies.

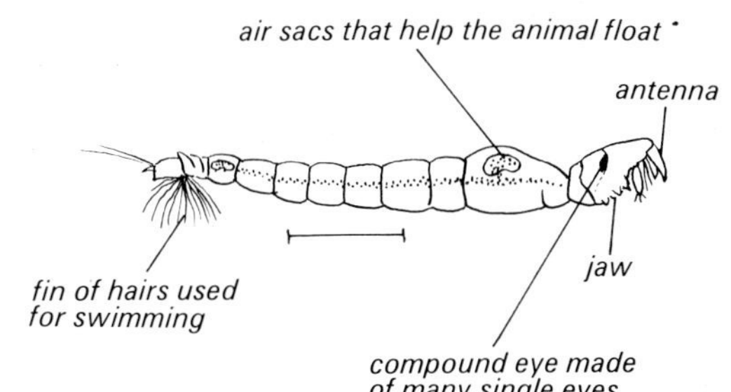

When gnat and midge larvae change into pupae they hang from the surface film of the water breathing through tubes. The adult flies escape from the pupal skin through the surface film of water.
They mate and the female lays eggs (see pages 22, 23).

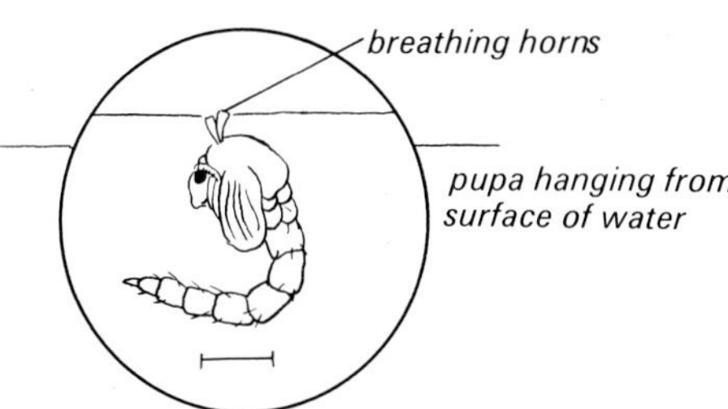

BLACK FLY LARVAE

Black fly larvae are common in some fast-flowing streams.

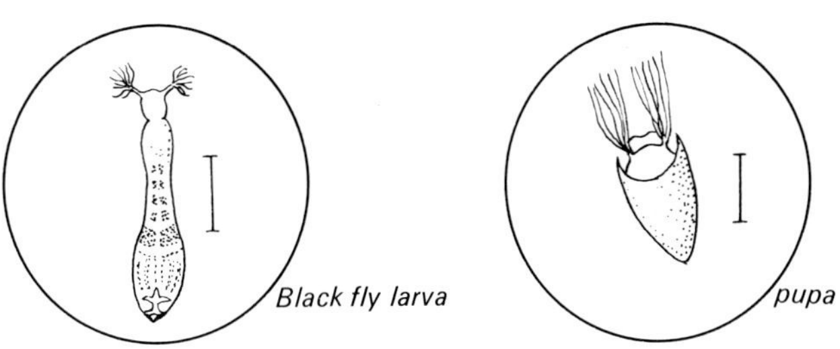

From page 15, clue 6

CHINA MARK MOTH CATERPILLARS and PUPAE

China Mark Moth caterpillars live in air-filled tubes under the leaves of water plants. They are herbivorous (see page 53). They feed by nibbling the leaf round the tube. The caterpillars pupate in the tube.

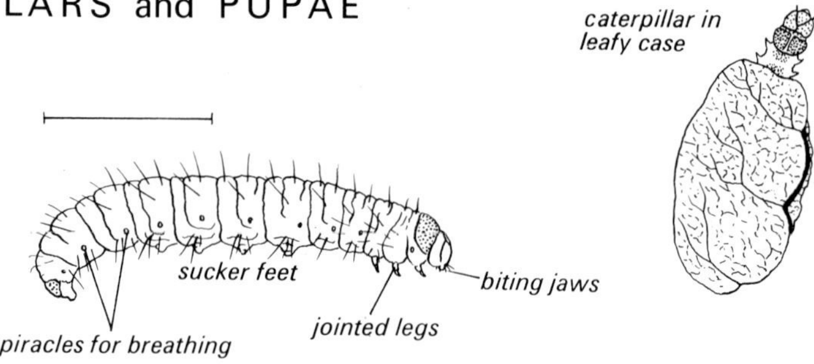

When the moths emerge they float to the surface of the water, fly away, mate and lay eggs on the underside of leaves in the water.

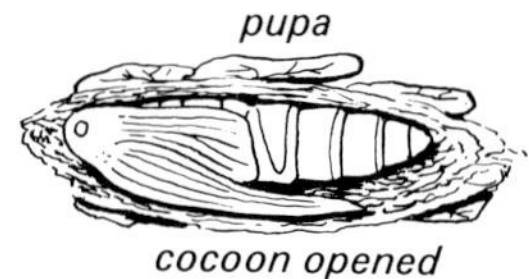

From page 17, clue 4.

DRONEFLY LARVAE

Dronefly larvae scavenge (see page 53) in the mud of stagnant pools. They float to the surface when they change into pupae.

After hatching and mating the females lay clusters of eggs (see page 23).

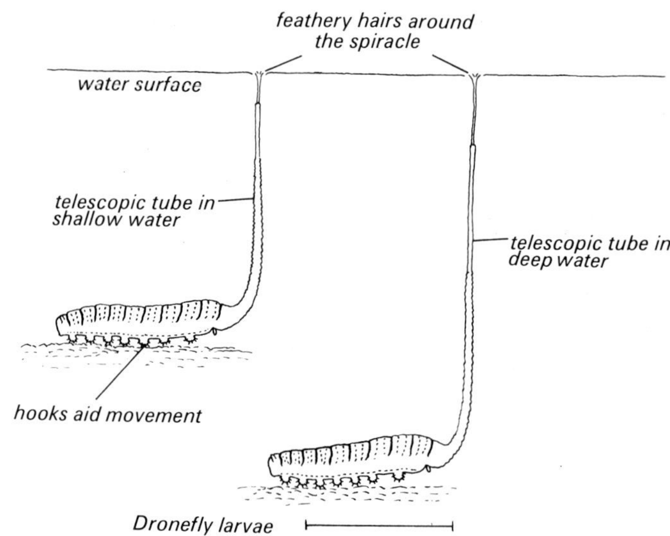

Dronefly larvae

CRAB GROUP (CRUSTACEA)

Most crustaceans shed their skins (moult) several times as they outgrow them. The new skin hardens after the animal has expanded. During this time damaged legs may also be regrown.

Many female crustaceans carry their eggs and young underneath their bodies, among their legs or swimmerets.

CRAYFISH

Crayfish may be found in streams hiding under stones, or in holes in the banks. They are carnivorous (see page 53) and hunt their prey at night. They are also scavengers (see page 53). Crayfish breathe through gills attached to the tops of their legs under the carapace.

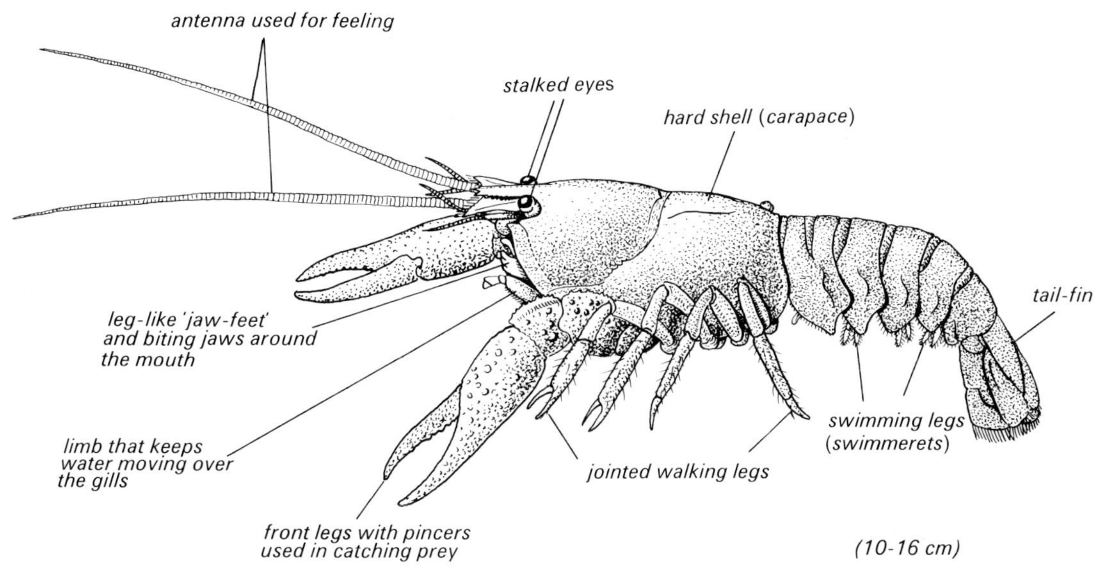

From page 16, clue 1

CRAB GROUP (CRUSTACEA)

FRESHWATER SHRIMPS

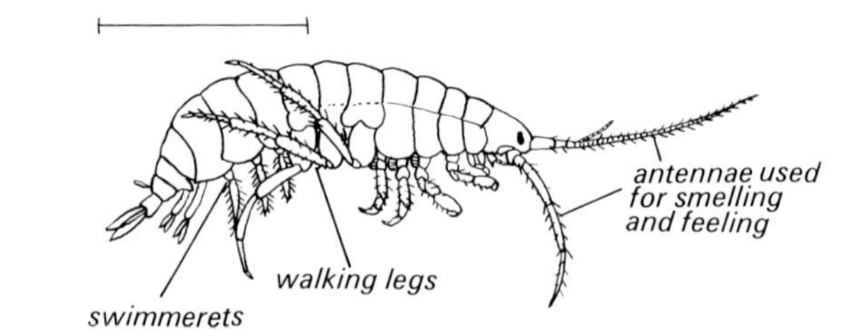

Freshwater shrimps live under stones or in mud in streams and ponds. They swim about on their sides scavenging (see page 53). They breathe through gills attached to the tops of their legs.
The females carry their eggs and young among the legs at the front of their bodies.

From page 16, clue 2

WATER SLATERS

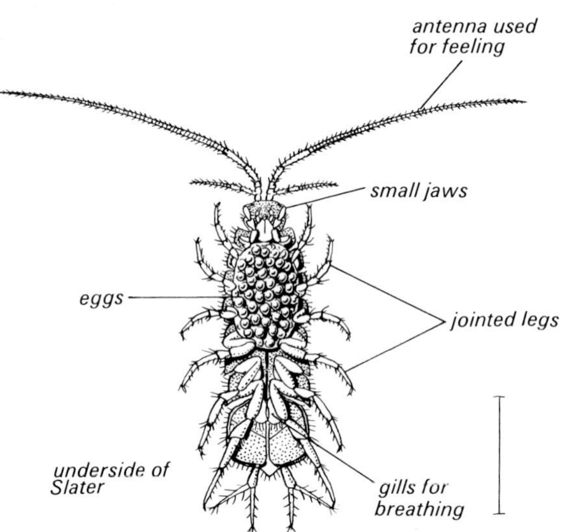

Water Slaters (Water Lice) live in weedy ponds or streams. Their bodies are flat. They scuttle along scavenging (see page 53) among plants.

From page 16, clue 3

FISH LICE

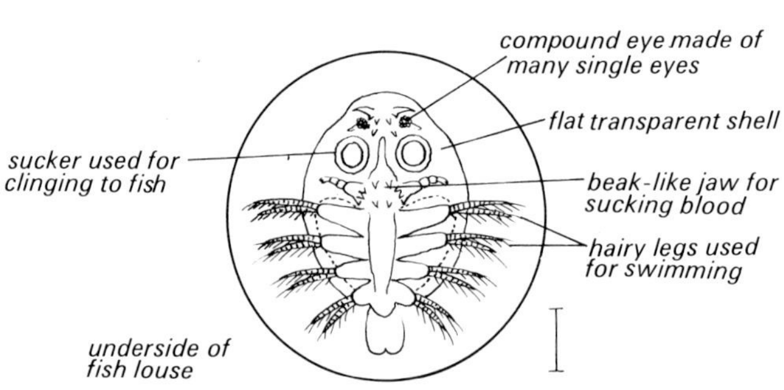

Fish Lice are very common parasites on fish. They cling to the fish and suck blood.

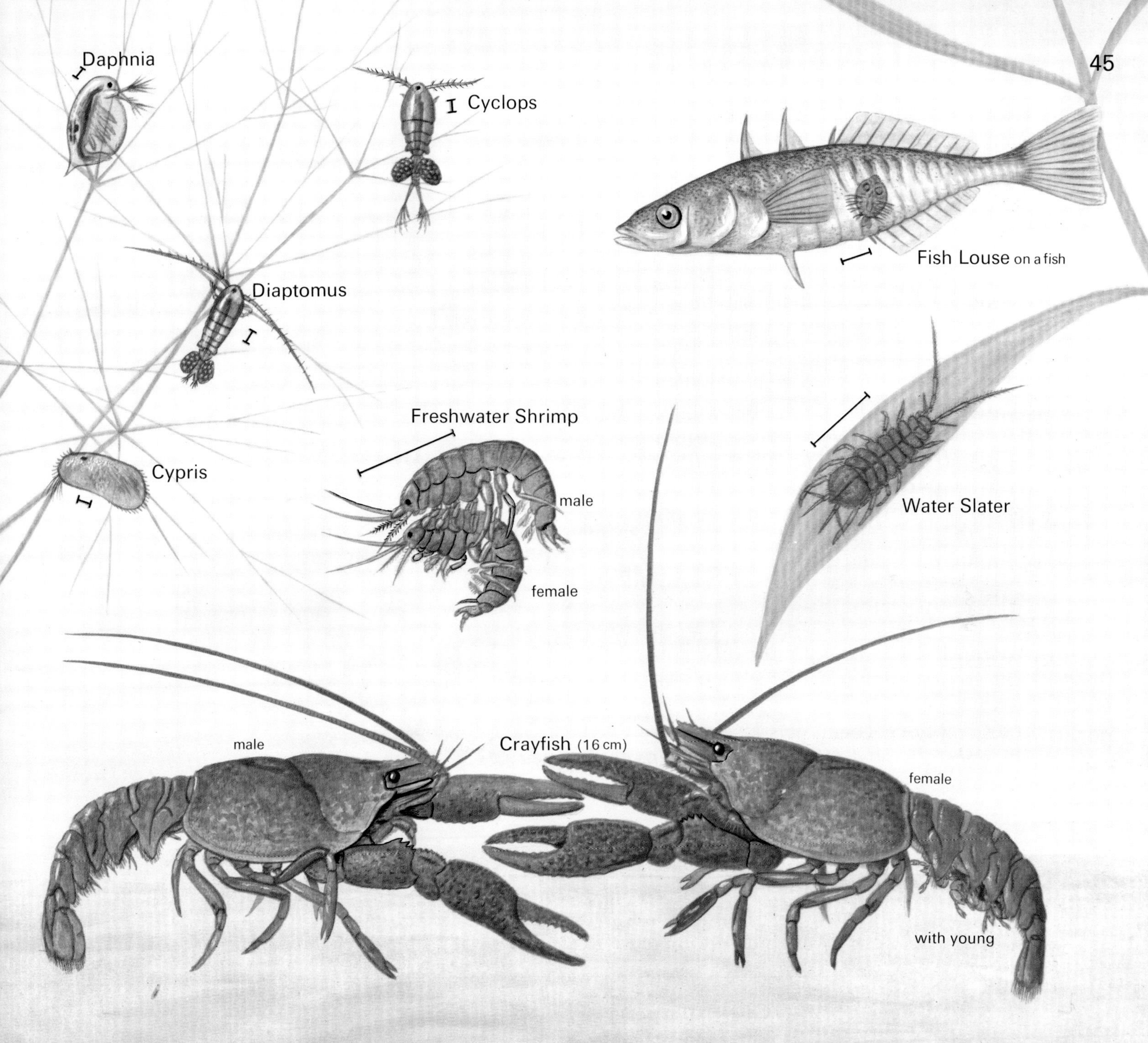
Daphnia
Cyclops
Diaptomus
Cypris
Freshwater Shrimp
male
female
Fish Louse on a fish
Water Slater
Crayfish (16 cm)
male
female
with young

From page 15, clues 1 and 2

SPIDERS and MITES (ARACHNIDA)

WATER SPIDERS

Water Spiders live in ponds and ditches. They are carnivorous (see page 53) and catch small pond animals which they take back to their webs to suck. Using silk from their spinnerets they build a flat web among water plants which they fill with air by collecting bubbles from the surface of the water and scraping the bubbles off their bodies under the web. When filled with air the web becomes bell-shaped. After mating the female spider adds a new web to the top of the bell and lays her eggs in it. After hatching the young spiders live for some time in the nest before escaping to catch their own food and collect a bubble of air.

spinnerets
spiracles for breathing
biting jaws
jaws
eyes
head from above
hind pair of legs and tip of abdomen break the surface film
water surface
bubble of air

From page 17, clue 3.

LEECHES

Leeches live in still and running water. Some leeches cling to other animals, pierce their skin, and suck blood.
The small Pond Leech eats insect larvae.
The eggs are most often laid in cocoons (see pages 23, 24).

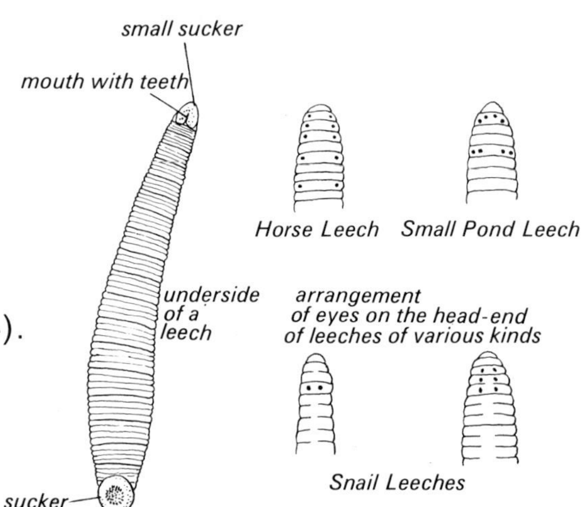

From page 18, clue 3

WORMS

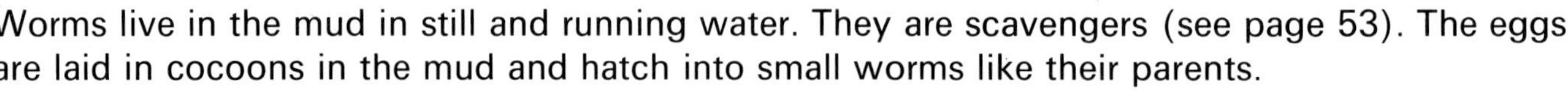
Worms live in the mud in still and running water. They are scavengers (see page 53). The eggs are laid in cocoons in the mud and hatch into small worms like their parents.

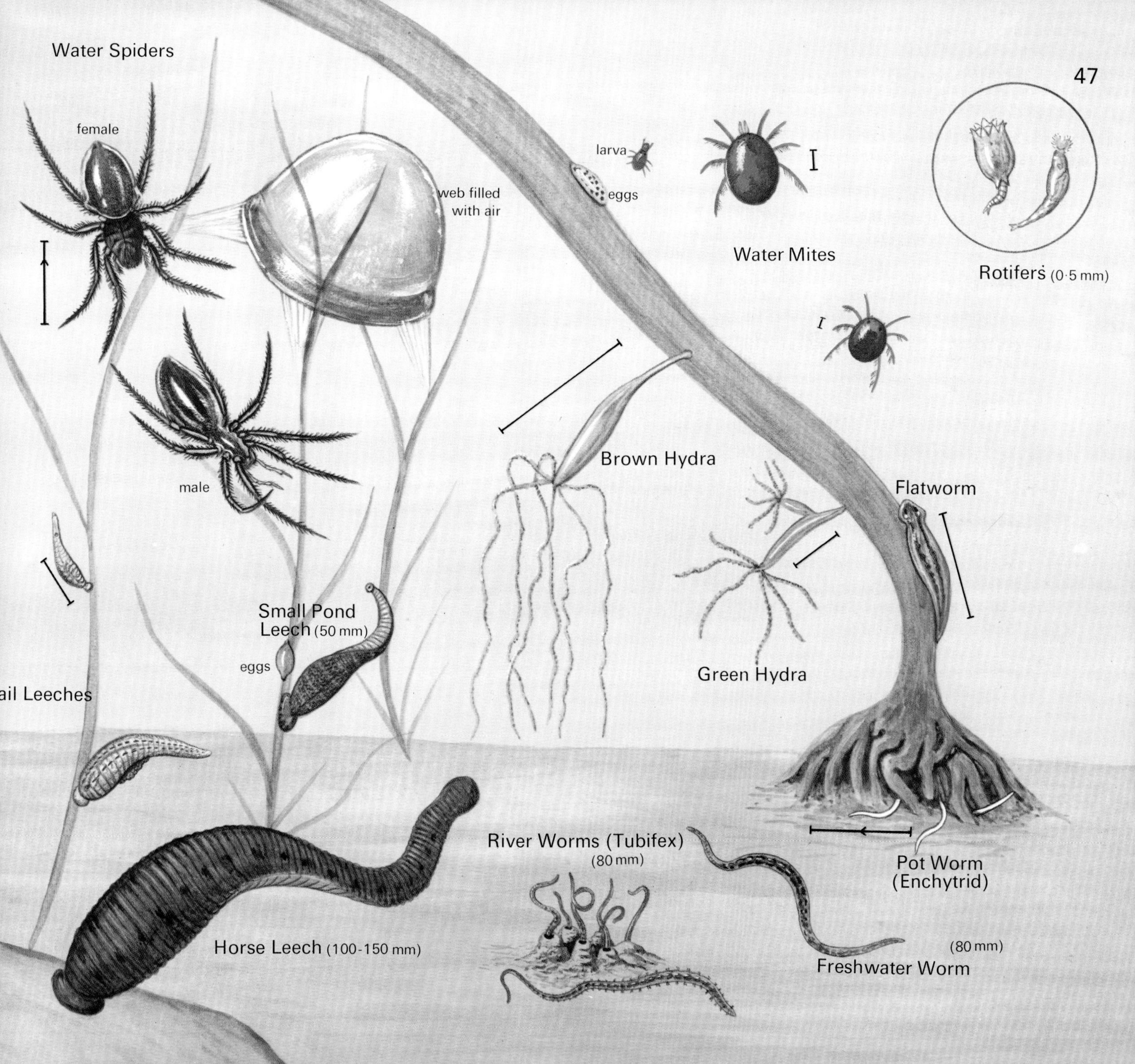
Water Spiders
female
male
web filled with air
larva
eggs
Water Mites
Rotifers (0·5 mm)
Brown Hydra
Green Hydra
Flatworm
ail Leeches
Small Pond Leech (50 mm)
eggs
Horse Leech (100-150 mm)
River Worms (Tubifex) (80 mm)
Pot Worm (Enchytrid)
(80 mm)
Freshwater Worm

 From page 20

SNAIL GROUP (MOLLUSCA)

Pond Snails, Bladder Snails, and Ramshorn Snails are all found in ponds, lakes and streams. Most of them are herbivores, and some are scavengers (see page 53) but the Great Pond Snail is a carnivore (see page 53).

All these snails have a long tongue, called a radula, covered with hundreds of teeth. As the front teeth wear out, the tongue and the teeth from behind move forward to take their places.

part of radula of carnivorous snail

part of radula of herbivorous snail

Pond snails breathe air by coming up to the surface of the water. They open their breathing holes through the surface film, expel the stale air from the lung cavity with a plopping sound, and collect fresh air. They close the opening before returning under water.

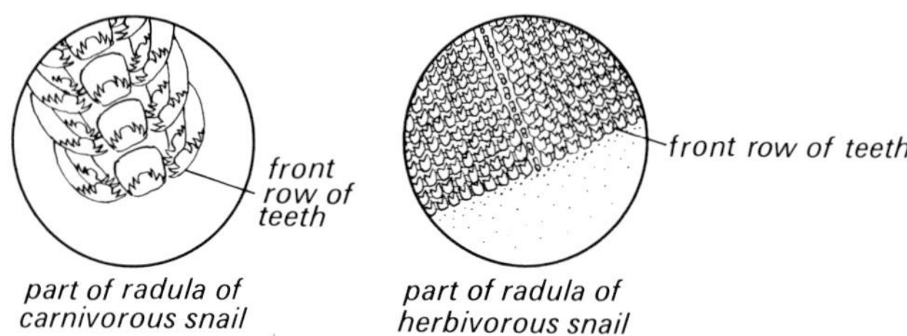

Freshwater Winkles and Valve Snails are similar to Pond Snails, but they breathe through gills in their lung cavity. When the snail is inside its shell the operculum closes the opening (see page 56).

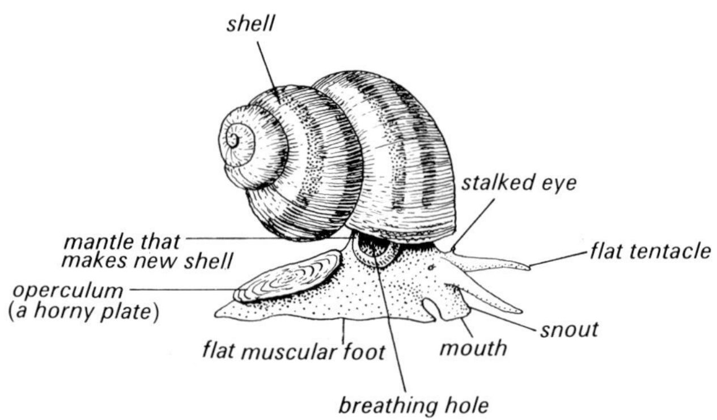

Most snails lay eggs after mating (see pages 22, 24).

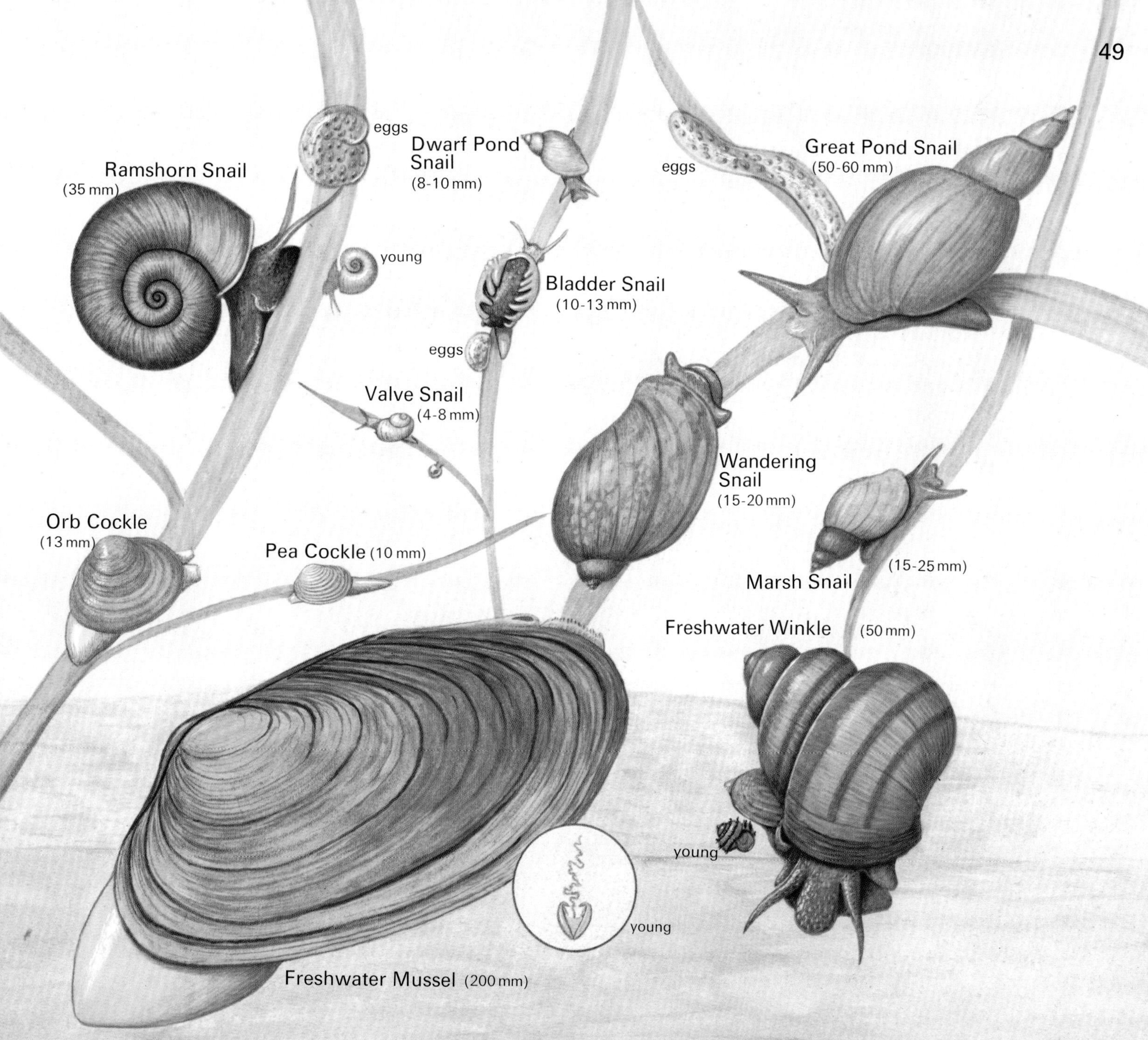
eggs
Dwarf Pond Snail
(8-10 mm)
Ramshorn Snail
(35 mm)
young
eggs
Great Pond Snail
(50-60 mm)
Bladder Snail
(10-13 mm)
eggs
Valve Snail
(4-8 mm)
Wandering Snail
(15-20 mm)
Orb Cockle
(13 mm)
Pea Cockle (10 mm)
(15-25 mm)
Marsh Snail
Freshwater Winkle
(50 mm)
young
young
Freshwater Mussel (200 mm)

From page 21

SNAIL GROUP (MOLLUSCA)

MUSSELS and COCKLES

Mussels and Cockles have two shells. They move about slowly on a wedge-shaped foot in the mud or sand at the bottom of the water.

As water is sucked in through the lower siphon it travels over the gills and out of the upper siphon; food is filtered from the water by hair-like cilia on the gills.

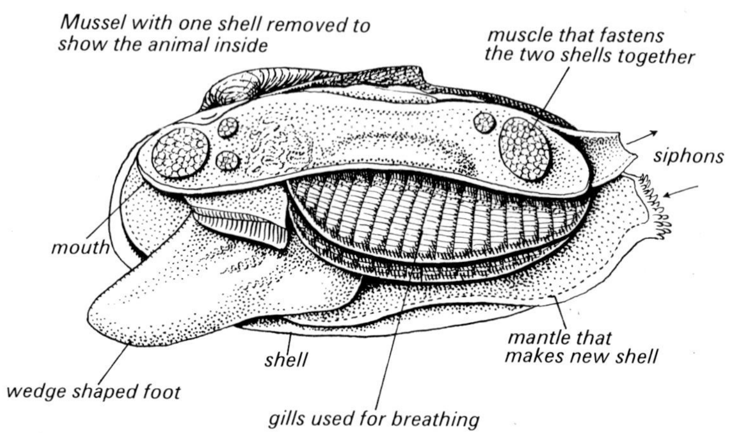

The eggs of Freshwater Mussels hatch into larvae among the gills of female mussels. The larvae pass out through the upper siphon and attach themselves to fish on which they feed until they become young mussels.

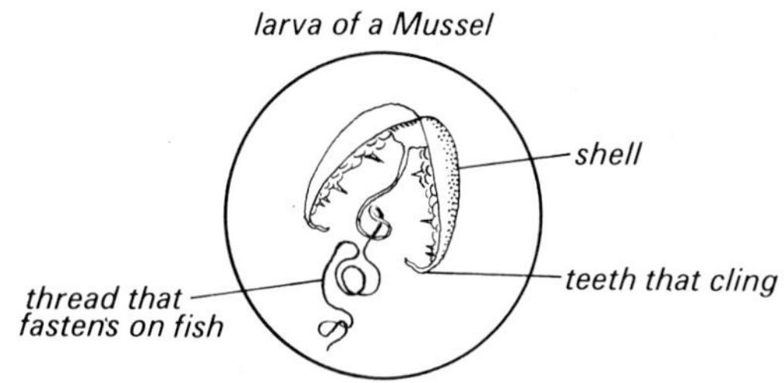

The eggs of Cockles hatch among the gills of the females into young, like their parents, and pass out through the upper siphon.

On pages 54, 55 you will find ideas for keeping and caring for the different kinds of freshwater animals.

Suggestions on pages 52, 56–58 will help you to make a study of the behaviour of the animals, and to keep records of your observations.

You can make your own book about freshwater animals and mount shed skins (see pages 4, 5), empty shells, and bones that you may find either in your aquariums or when you are collecting animals. Some of them may be mounted on paper under clear self-adhesive plastic, and others stuck in small boxes and covered with cellophane for protection.

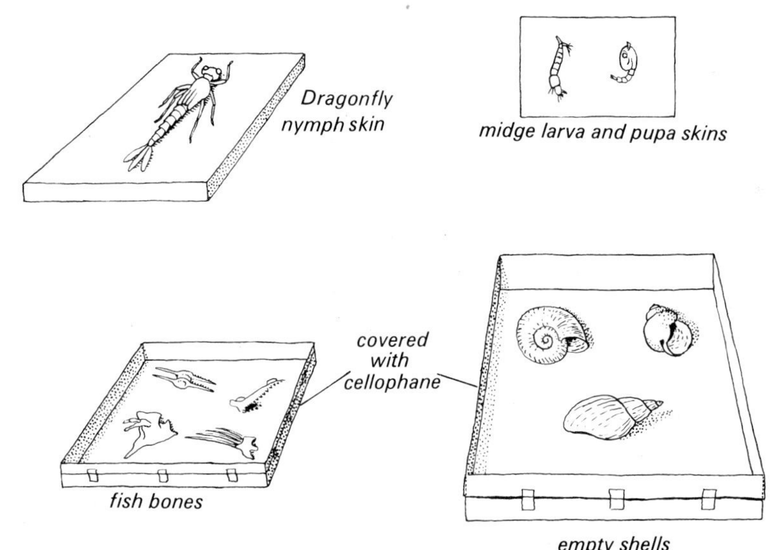

Frog, toad, or newt skins may be mounted like this.

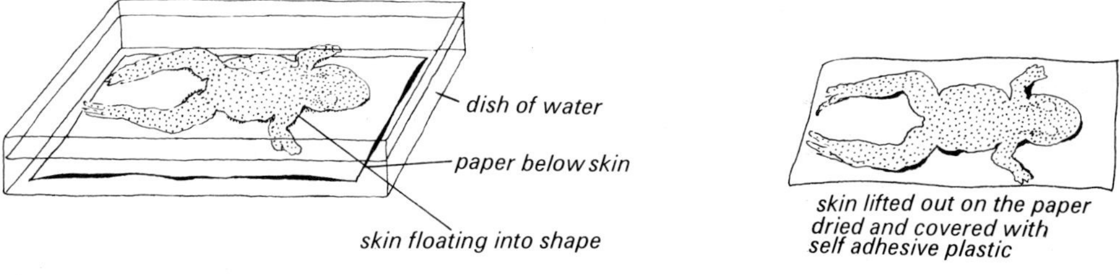

You can find out in which particular part of the water your animals prefer to live by drawing a map of the area in which you are collecting, and plotting on it the places where you found the animals (see below).

1. Lesser Water Boatman
2. Water Fleas
3. Mayfly Nymphs
4. Tadpoles
5. Fish seen resting nose to bank after dark

You can work out whether the animals are found:
1. in different places at different times of the day
2. in different places at different times of the year
3. in sunlight or shadow
4. in places where plants are growing or in open water
5. in the warmer or colder parts of the water.

What other things can you find out about the way the animals behave in a pond?

Keep a weekly record of the temperature of water in the pond and of the air above it (see graph).

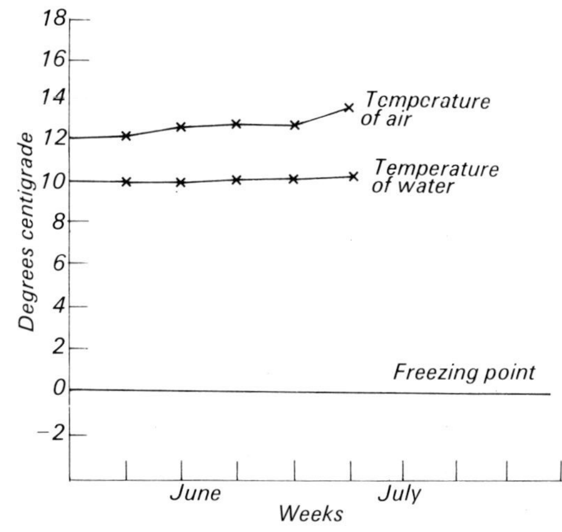

Plants and animals all need food in order to grow. Because plants are green they make food from water and the gas that every living thing breathes out (carbon dioxide). Sunlight supplies the energy which green leaves use to re-group the atoms in water and carbon dioxide to turn them into sugar.
In plants sugar is turned into starch, fats, oils, and proteins.

Animals eat this ready-made food.
Some of them eat plants; they are called HERBIVORES.
Others eat other animals; they are called CARNIVORES.

Animals called SCAVENGERS eat dead plants and animals. Decaying plants and animals are broken down into food products which can be used again by green plants to make proteins.

The illustration below shows the food eaten by some of the herbivores, carnivores, and scavengers which live in freshwater. This is often called a '*food web*'.

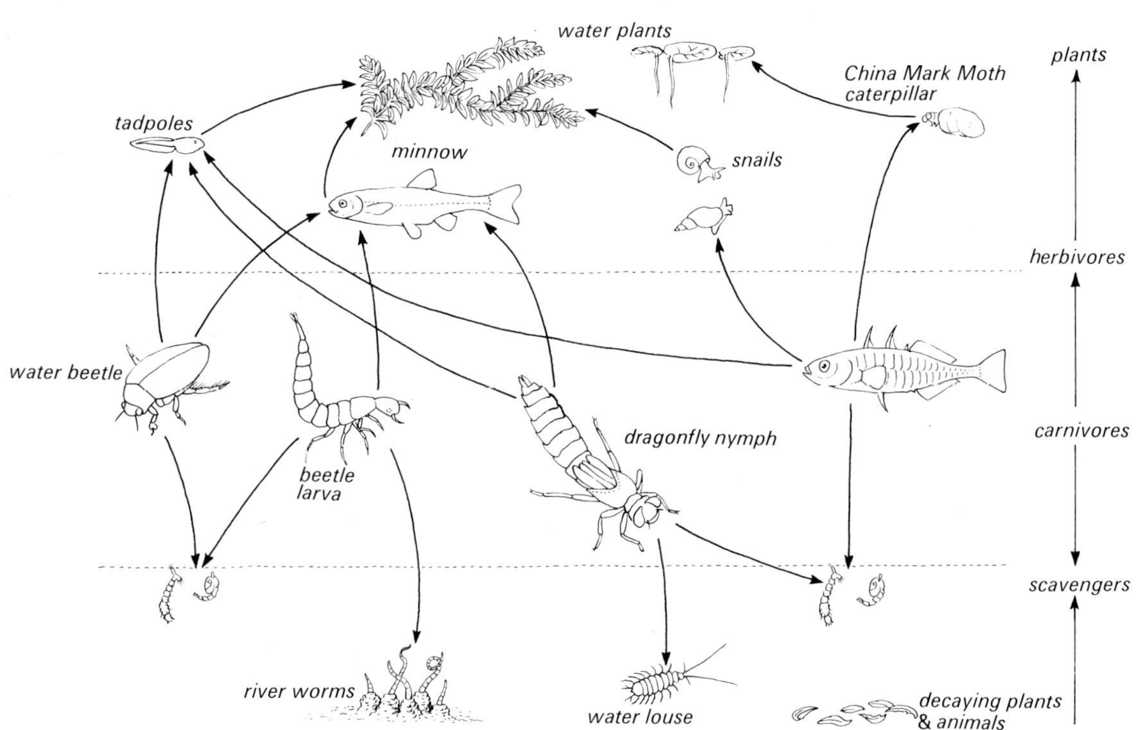

HOW TO SET UP AQUARIUMS (artificial ponds and tanks)

All aquariums need to be set up several days before you wish to use them.

If you are keeping animals indoors you will need either a glass or plastic tank

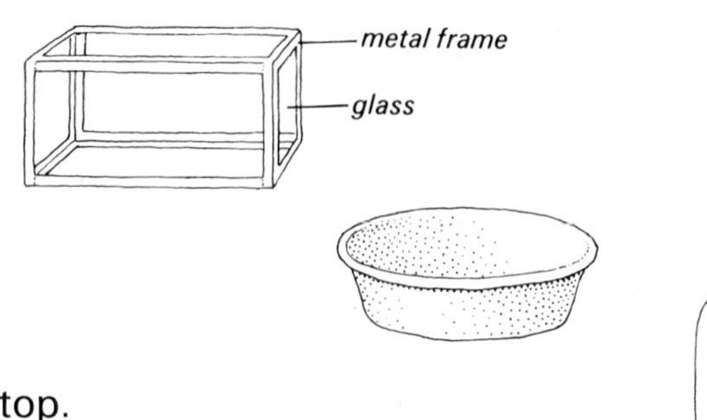

or a white plastic bowl

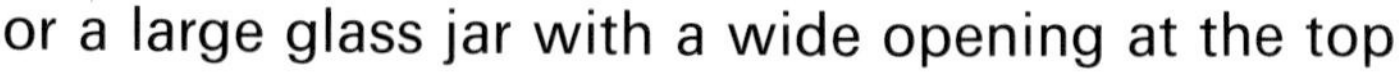

or a large glass jar with a wide opening at the top.

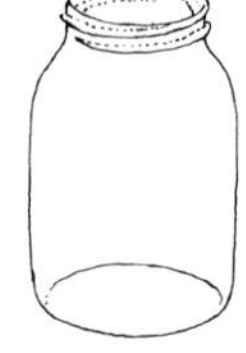

If you are keeping animals outside you will need an old kitchen sink, or a hole in the ground lined with strong plastic.

AQUARIUM for TADPOLES, SMALL FROGS, and NEWTS

Newts and small frogs will need a lid of perforated zinc.

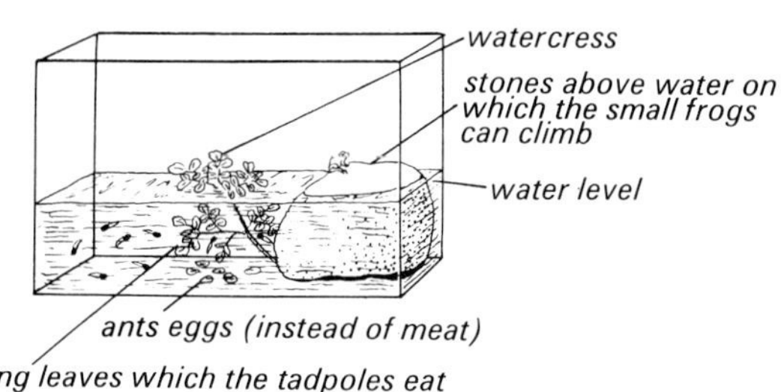

AQUARIUM for BEETLE LARVAE

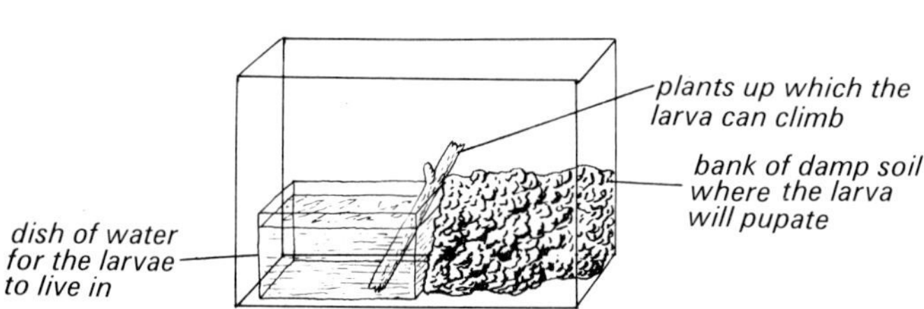

AQUARIUM for DRAGONFLY and DAMSELFLY NYMPHS

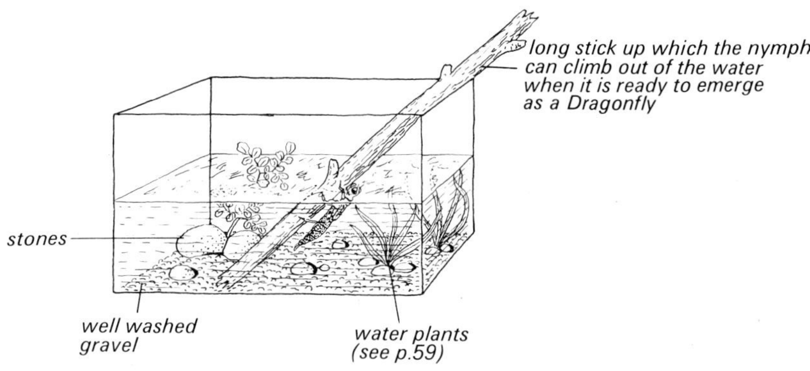

AQUARIUM for other FRESHWATER ANIMALS

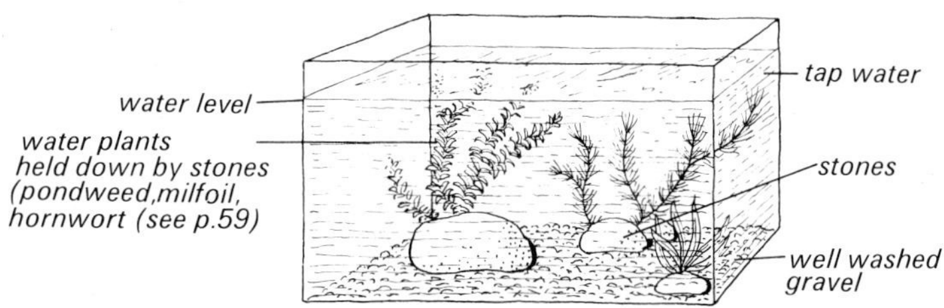

Feeding the animals

HERBIVOROUS animals (see page 53) eat the plants in the aquarium.

CARNIVOROUS animals (see page 53) can be fed on ant pupae (sold in pet shops as ants eggs), waterfleas, tubifex and whiteworm; all may be bought in pet shops.

Remember that carnivorous animals will eat other animals that are in the aquarium with them.

SCAVENGERS (see page 53) scavenge dead plants and animals on the bottom of the aquarium. They help to keep the aquarium clean.

Animals that live in water either take oxygen from the water when they breathe, or rise to the surface and collect a bubble of air through the surface film. Watch your animals carefully to see which they do. You may like to record your findings like this, or think of another way.

animals that come to the surface to breathe	*animals that do not rise to the surface to breathe*

When freshwater animals breathe they take oxygen from the air or water and give off carbon dioxide into it, through their skin, spiracles, or gills.

They need the oxygen to combine with digested food in muscles, bone, and nerves to provide energy for movement and growth. The food is changed into carbon dioxide and water which are breathed out.

Gills of fish, tadpoles, and snails have blood capillaries (very small blood vessels) and are called VASCULAR GILLS. Blood corpuscles flowing through the capillaries collect oxygen from the water.

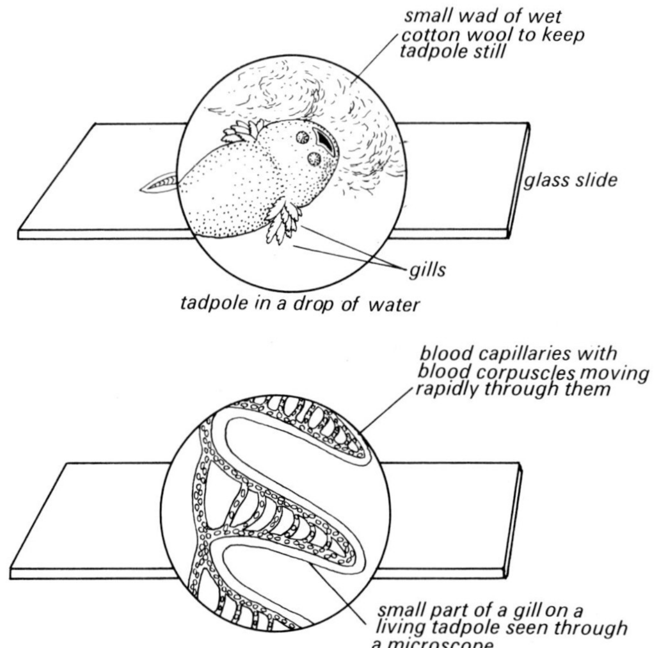

If you look at the gills of a tadpole, the skin of a tadpole's tail, or the web of a frog's foot under a microscope, you will be able to see the corpuscles moving through the capillaries.

Gills of insects, called TRACHEAL GILLS, have air-tubes which collect oxygen from the water.

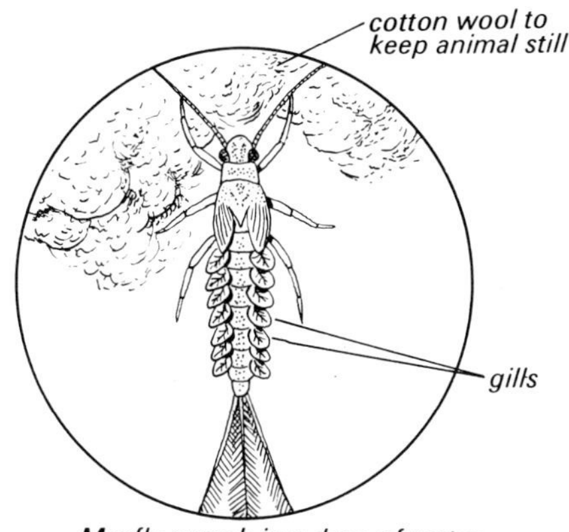

Mayfly nymph in a drop of water

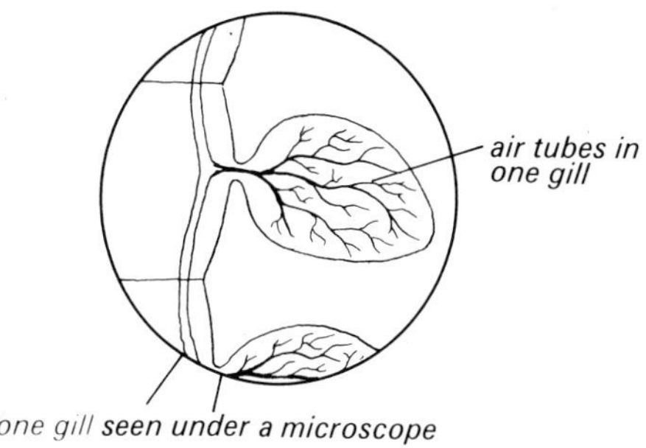

one gill seen under a microscope

Some animals come to the surface to exchange air through air tubes in their tail filaments or horns. Others collect it as a bubble over their hairy bodies; it passes into air-tubes in the body through holes called SPIRACLES.

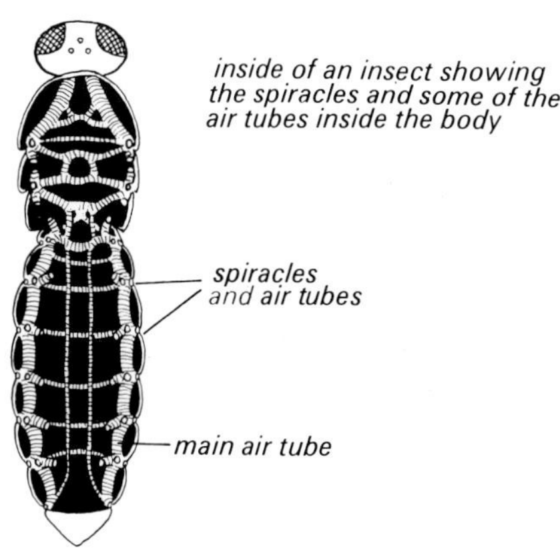

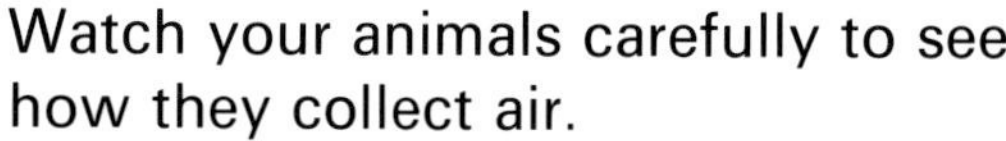

Watch your animals carefully to see how they collect air.

Record what you see like this or think of another way.

animals that collect air through tail filaments or horns	animals that collect air in an air bubble	animals that collect air some other way

Many animals swim; they push against the water in order to move forward.

Watch the animals you have found to see how they push against the water. You may like to record your findings like this or think of another way.

name of animal	*how it pushes against the water*

Many animals have streamlined bodies in order to move easily through the water. Which of your animals are streamlined?

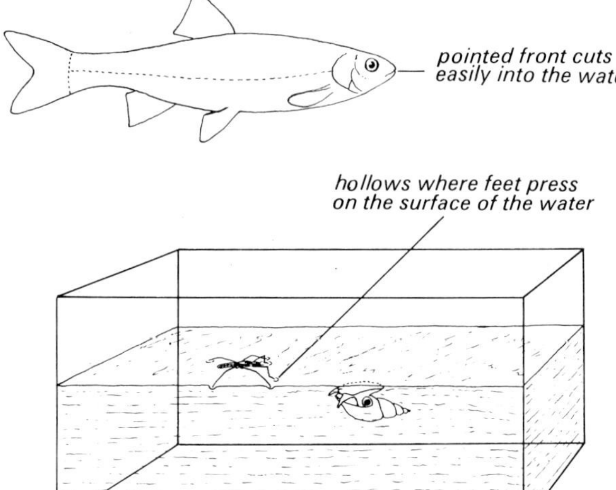

Pond Skaters and other animals move about on the surface of the water which seems to have a skin; snails often glide along underneath it.

Make a list of pond animals that seem to float to the top unless they swim hard or cling to plants to keep themselves down.
Do these animals have a bubble of air around their bodies?

Watch a fish using its fins and tail to change direction as it swims. How does it do this?

SOME PLANTS THAT WILL GROW IN YOUR AQUARIUMS (see page 54)

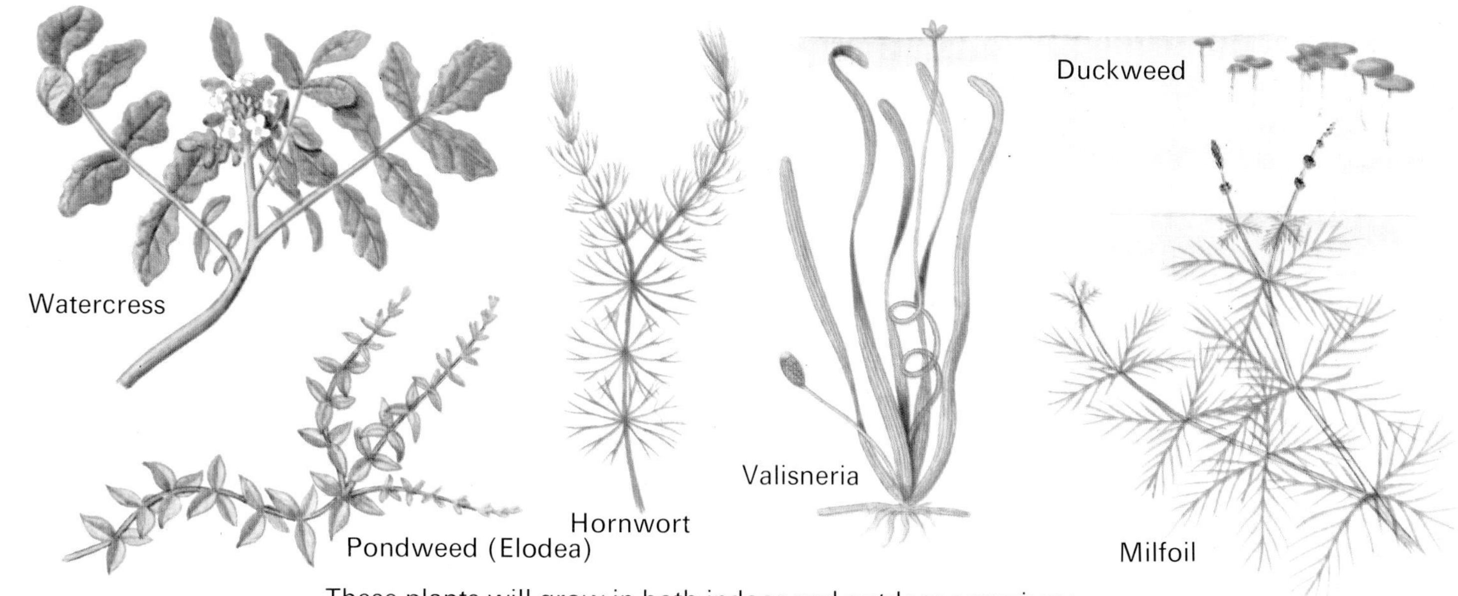

Watercress
Pondweed (Elodea)
Hornwort
Valisneria
Duckweed
Milfoil

These plants will grow in both indoor and outdoor aquariums

Waterlily
Arrowhead
Bogbean
Rushes

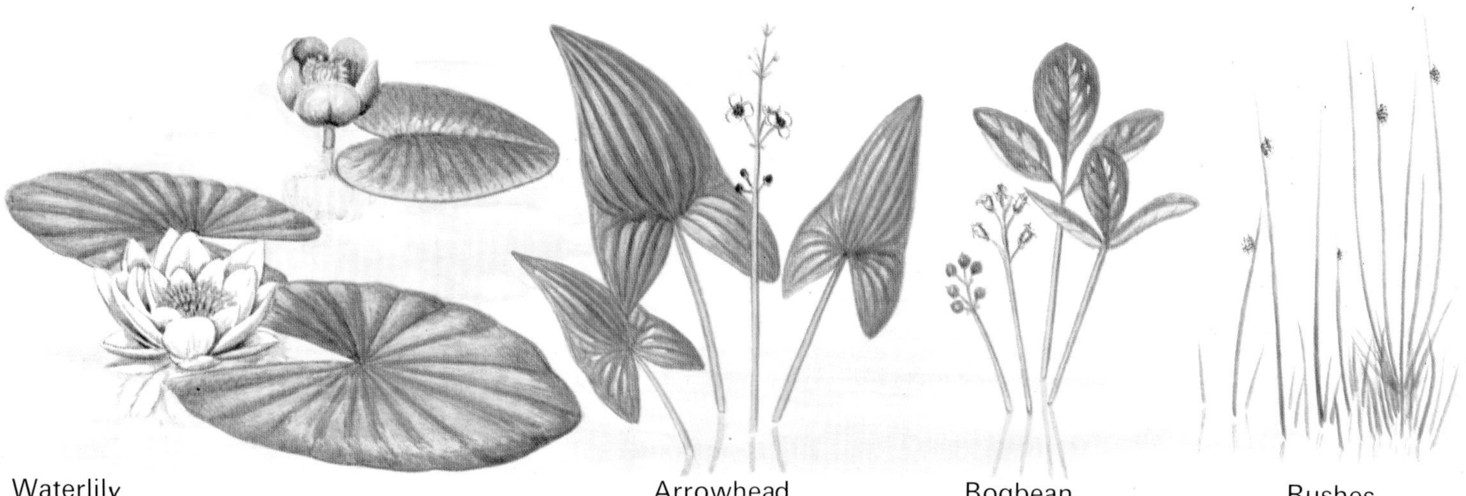

These plants will only grow in outdoor aquariums

Green plants in aquariums produce oxygen which animals need when they breathe (see page 56).

All eyes have a lens like the one that can be removed from the eye of a fish. The lens produces an image, on the back of the eye, of whatever is in front of it.
If you use the lens from the eye of a large fish you can project the image of a candle onto a screen.

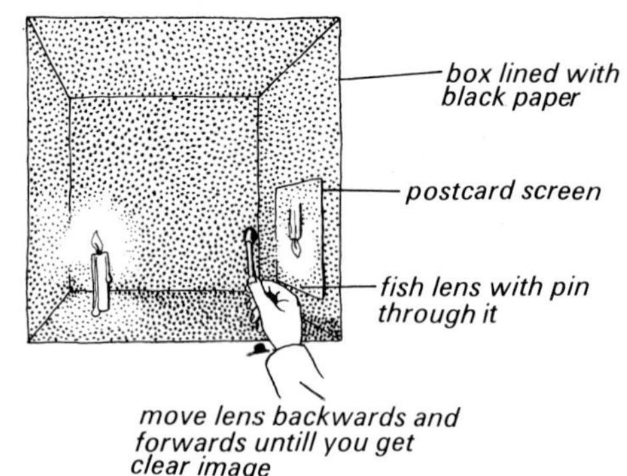

(The head of a large fish bought from a fishmonger will also be useful for seeing details of gills and scales.)

A Caddis larva may be persuaded to come out of its case by gently pushing the *blunt* end of a pin in at the tail end.
If it is put into a dish with small pieces of paper and leaves or small stones it will probably build itself a new case.

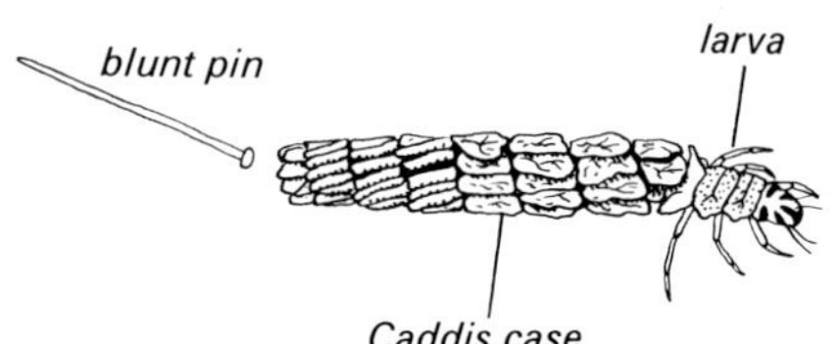

Bibliography

Clegg, John, *Observer's Book of Pond Life* (Warne)
The Freshwater Life of the British Isles (Warne)
Englehardt, W., *Pond-life* (The young specialist looks at) (Burke)
Haworth, F. M., *Aquaria* (University of London Press)
Pond Dwellers (University of London Press)
Janus, H., *Molluscs* (The young specialist looks at) (Burke)
McInnes, J., *Making and Keeping Aquaria* (Ward, Lock)
Travis, Jenkins A., *The Fishes of the British Isles* (Warne)

Index